A FARRIER'S TALES

A FARRIER'S TALES

Frank Morris

ATHENA PRESS
LONDON

ISBN 1 84401 589 0

First Published 2005 by
ATHENA PRESS
Queen's House, 2 Holly Road
Twickenham TW1 4EG
United Kingdom

Printed for Athena Press

Introduction

I was planning to retire at the end of March 2003 — the end of the tax year — when my mobile forge was smashed up in a road accident. This was towards the end of February, and the damage was such that there was no point in even trying to repair it in the time that I had left, so I retired there and then. I felt very sorry for my customers, who I had to abandon at such short notice; but there was nothing I could do about it, and, under the circumstances, my customers were as sorry for me as I was for them. I had almost completed fifty-three years as a blacksmith and farrier, so I considered that I had done my share of the national workload.

There was no romantic start to my career as a farrier. It wasn't that I loved horses so much that I had to work with them; it was more that I was eager to leave school, and told my father that I wanted to be a farmer. He said, 'Tha can ferget abaht that till tha can afford thi own farm. Tha wants a proper apprenticeship, so that tha hes summat to fall back on if jobs get scarce.' He came home one night from work and said to me, 'Go see So-and-so i' Bingla [Bingley], I've got thi a job as an apprentice blacksmith, an' tha can start straight off.'

So I became apprentice blacksmith at a firm of general engineers, who specialised in making foundry equipment, and one of my jobs was to keep the store lockers topped up with small forgings, like pipe holdfasts, ha'penny headed holdfasts, clothes line hooks, gutter brackets and sundry items that joiners, plumbers and builders used. Making these items was an essential part of training in the use of hand tools, but after making a gross of one item, then a gross of another, I soon became conversant with the tools of the trade.

I moved on to learn shoeing horses and agricultural blacksmithing, which I found a lot more interesting than my previous job, but I found the shoeing very hard work. Although the horse was on the decline for general use in early 1950s, we shod quite a variety, from shires to Shetland ponies, and as you read through these stories, you will come to know what I really think of the latter — and why.

After completing my apprenticeship, I went back into foundry equipment-making, because the pay was quite a bit better, and having married, I needed all the money I could get — you know how it is. It was then that I was asked by an acquaintance if I knew how to shoe horses. I said I did, and he asked me to do one for him. I hadn't done one for quite a few years and the shoeing muscles had disappeared, and the cutting tools that he provided were so unbelievably blunt that it took me two evenings' work to shoe the one horse — and I had never been so worn out in my life! Anyway, the chap was very pleased with the result, and told me that I should be shoeing for a living, as horse owners were crying out for farriers.

I thought about it for a while, and finally decided to give it a go. I put an advert in the local paper, and had quite a few enquiries, and I would go out after work and shoe two or three at night. One day, I arrived home and my wife said that she had taken out a three-month contract for an ad in the *Yorkshire Post*.

Well, the telephone never stopped ringing, with enquiries from all over Yorkshire, from Scarborough to Huddersfield, and all places in between. We (my wife and I) decided that I must take the plunge, and start up on my own account, and it turned out to be the best thing I ever did. In fact we wished we could cancel the contract with the *Yorkshire Post* after a couple of weeks, because there was far more work than I could even hope to cope with. I would set off at seven o'clock in the morning, and get home up to nine o'clock at night, six days a week, and, as I was shoeing eight or ten horses a day, I soon got muscled up to the job with this workload. Even though I worked extremely hard, I began to really enjoy my work — mostly, as not all our equine friends are particularly friendly, especially when they aren't very well handled; and as some of my stories indicate, life as a farrier is not all beer and skittles.

THE JOB: FARRIERY

Farriery is not just about putting shoes on horses. It also entails looking after the feet by trimming the hooves in a proper manner, thus ensuring the proper alignment of the bones of the leg. The front feet should be trimmed to an angle of approximately forty-five degrees, whilst the hind feet should be about fifty degrees, and the heels must be level. If these criteria are observed at all times, a horse will stay sound throughout its life — apart from accidental injuries; but if they are not observed, a horse can become unsound to downright lame, and can be subject to insidious, chronic lameness, such as navicular disease, ringbone, sidebone, suspensory ligament and deep flexor tendon damage, which often appear in its later life.

Horse shoeing is a very hard, physical job, and quite often a dangerous job, but it is also a very skilful job, which requires a great deal of concentration. There is also an artistic side to it, as a farrier has to be able to make a shoe from memory without measuring it. By the time the feet have been dressed, the shape of both front and hind feet should be memorised, and the shoes made to fit very nearly at the first time of trying. Only a slight alteration should be required to produce a perfect fit, which is essential for the nails to be driven in the proper place. If the nails do not go in exactly the right place, this can result in lameness, or cause the horn to split, resulting in lost shoes, and pieces breaking away from the hoof.

I have often thought that a farrier needs to have the strength of Samson, the courage of a lion, the patience of Job, a thick skin, tin legs and – quite often – another pair of hands, in order to hold onto a leg and nail a shoe on the foot.

It is always difficult shoeing a young horse for the first couple of times, but if the owners do their homework on them, the trauma is reduced considerably. In my experience, the most trouble comes from owners overfeeding their animals – or 'injudicious feeding', as I once heard it described. This can make even the quietest of horses into a bundle of dynamite, just waiting for a farrier to start work on it before it explodes. Quite a few of my stories involve overfed, underworked and scarcely handled animals, and although the stories sound funny after the event, I can assure you that they were anything but funny at the time! In a few of these episodes, I show how I used to deal with some of these situations, and if your farrier ever asks you to make him a cup of tea at a crucial time, you will know why.

All of these tales are taken from actual situations, with facilities – or lack of facilities, more often than not – described where necessary. All the conversations actually took place – not in these exact words, as some things happened thirty years ago, but some of the lines and comments are actually reproduced word for word. I will leave you, the reader, to decide which is which.

The Horse Owner

One of my favourite sayings is, 'I can manage the horses, it's the owners I can't cope with.' Not all owners fall into this category, as some are extremely understanding. Indeed, some are even sympathetic; but many owners seem to think that horses are born being shod, and, if they are difficult, it's the farrier's fault.

There are the owners who say, 'It's its first time, and I must have it done quietly.' Then I would say, 'Well, have you told the horse?' and they would look at me as if I'd suddenly appeared from outer space, and say, 'What do you mean?'

I would then respond, 'I have not come here for a punch-up, only to shoe your horse, and your horse will decide how quietly the job gets done – so have you told the horse?' I never seemed to get on with these women (yes, they are always women)… I wonder why?

Then there are the parents who say, 'We've bought a three-year-old for our daughter [who is five] so that they can grow up together' – all together… *Ahhhhh!* How naive can you get?

Then there are those who say, 'It's only a baby, and I don't want it spoiling.' Well, in my book, there are no babies; if people want their horses shoeing, then they must ensure that they are ready to be shod. As far as I'm concerned, these horses are already spoiled, and whenever I heard this phrase, I would groan to myself and think, *Oh ma gawd, not another!*

There are the owners who stand there watching to see that you don't raise your voice and frighten the poor creature, and there are those who say, 'I haven't slept since I phoned you, I hope you will be all right.' To these women (yes, again, they are always women) I would say, 'Look, don't worry, both your horse and I will be fine.' They were always very nice people.

Then there are those who own a horse that is a bit of a slug, and is boring to ride, so they proceed to stuff it with oats until it is thoroughly addle-brained, making it a danger to all concerned with it — especially the poor farrier. I remember one beast in particular that was normally stone quiet, until the owner stuffed it with food, and the next time I went to shoe it, it jumped straight over the owner, who was holding it, and over a wall of hay bales stacked three high! If people want to get themselves hurt, that's fine with me, but they should remember that they will need the animal shoeing at some stage, and should not make a farrier's job any more difficult and dangerous than it already is. OK, so I'm whingeing, but these stories are told from the farrier's point of view, and I carry scars to prove the point.

There was one owner who bought a big dressage horse that wouldn't be tied up, and was a swine to shoe. She kept it at one of my livery yards, and I told her that whenever her horse was on the shoeing list, she must come at least an hour before her shoeing time, and give the horse a good lunging (exercise on a long rein) before I attempted to shoe it. This strategy proved to be sound, as the horse behaved reasonably well after a good lunging, and shoeing was made a lot easier.

One day, when this horse was to shoe, the owner turned up early and took it out to lunge. When her time arrived, she brought the horse into the shoeing box, and I made a start in my usual way, not expecting any trouble. The horse, however, had other ideas, and it started by booting me across the box. I went back to it and tried again, and the same thing happened again, so I asked the owner if she had given it its usual lunging. She said, 'Yes, but it didn't want to trot, so I just let it walk round.'

I said, 'In that case, you can let it just walk back to its box, and you can have another day off work next week.' She wasn't very pleased, but she made sure that the horse was well lunged in future.

The best owners were those who would have the horse ready when I arrived, and say, 'There you are, I'll leave you to get on.' Then, after a while, they'd bring out a cup of tea. I always knew there would be no trouble at these places.

To the majority of owners with well-behaved animals, I must say that it was always a pleasure to work for you, and but for you, the job of horse shoeing would not be worth having.

The Horses

Horses, of course, come in all shapes and sizes, from shires and Clydesdales to Miniature Shetlands, and all manner of equine types in between. However, they all have one thing in common, and that is, they never like being shod. Fortunately, the majority come to accept the process — if only grudgingly — and the rest range from niggly to downright nasty — and again, all manner of behaviour in between. Some respond to just being 'muscled' — that is, held onto, until they decide that you are not about to give in. Some respond to being shouted at and 'muscled', some need a quick poke in the ribs, some need the twitch, and some need a good hiding, and some are not even fit to go near, let alone to shoe.

I think that my stories cover just about the whole range of equine behaviour, and I have tried to be, at least, reasonably honest in my descriptions of the situations. Unfortunately, a great many people seem to think that horses are accustomed to being shod from birth and that farriers spoil them. The real fact is that owners who don't do their homework on their horses, like picking their legs up and tapping their feet regularly, or the owners who overfeed their animals, or the owners who only ride their horses once a week — these are the people who spoil them.

Horses are herding animals, and are not keen on being separated from their mates, especially when they have been running out together for a long time — like hunters in summer — and if they are brought straight out of the field when the farrier arrives to shoe them, they need another horse to stand with them for company, or they can be extremely difficult to deal with.

Probably the most consistently badly behaved are brood stock, Shetland ponies and donkeys — not necessarily in that order. Brood stock are tricky because quite often they are just turned out in a field and left to get on with the job of multiplying, and are rarely, if ever, handled. Shetlands, because they are never broken in or handled to any great extent; in fact, the nearest they come to being broken in is when an owner sits a child on its back, and if the pony doesn't chuck the child off, it's considered to be broken in! They very rarely have their feet picked up, and then the owners wonder why the farrier has difficulty trimming the feet, and even more difficulty if they need shoeing. Donkeys are difficult because often they are only used instead of the owner buying a lawnmower, and are never touched from one visit of the farrier to the next. Quite a few of my stories are about brood stock and Shetland ponies, as these animals seem to provide all the fun.

There are no tales to tell of the well-behaved horses — the vast majority — as they seem quite boring in comparison with the above. The most interesting thing about these horses is dealing with any lameness, and a few of my stories are about this subject. These tales are all based on actual situations, and are told strictly from the farrier's point of view... for a change.

The Mule

A chap once rang to ask if I would go to his place and trim the feet of a mule. I had never had anything to do with mules before, and didn't know what shape their feet were supposed to be, or what sort of behaviour to expect, although I had no doubt the foot shape would take care of itself, with a bit of common sense. When I arrived, I found the mule was not much bigger than a St Bernard dog, and its feet were teacup size, although somewhat overgrown. There were four of us men there to handle it, indeed, there were enough of us to eat it, so the job looked like being a bit of a doddle. There was the owner, who must have weighed nineteen stones, another chap who weighed at least sixteen stones, and another fellow about the same size as me, about thirteen stones — although I would not be holding, just trimming.

So we started with just the owner holding the pint-sized mule. But no sooner had I got a foot off the floor, than there was a scuffle, and the mule jumped over the low wall (the boskin front) of the mistal where we were working. The two biggest men just got hold of it and lifted it back over (that's how small it was), and we set to again, this time with the big guys holding this fearsome creature down.

There was another kerfuffle, and the mule escaped the hold of the heavy gang, and jumped over the wall again. It was duly retrieved, and this time all three of the men got to grips with the little beast. There was one with his arm over its neck, another lying over its back from one side, and the other over its back from the other side; in fact I reckoned there was about forty-eight stones of men holding this tiny mule down! As soon as I tried to pick up a foot, it did a quick shimmy, and disappeared over the boskin front again, and when I looked up, there were these three men still in the positions they were in before the mule did its disappearing act. It was a bit like a charade, you know — 'Guess what we were just doing!'

By this time the owner was getting a bit miffed that they couldn't hold this small animal down, but I thought, *We've got to have a fresh act here, or we'll never get this job done.* So I tied the mule to the cow-tying stake and said, 'Right, let's see you get over the wall now!'

It tried, oh, how it tried, but it couldn't get away from the cow tie, and I was able to hold on, it being so small, whilst it struggled, and I soon had the job done. That was a valuable lesson learned: it doesn't matter how big the men are who are holding onto even the smallest of our equine friends, you can't beat tying them to an immovable object, as some of my other stories will confirm.

The Day I Got the Hump

I got a call from a circus asking if I would go and see to their horses' feet. They said that they were leaving the following day, and could I come straight away. I asked how many horses were involved and they said, 'A couple or so.' Well, I had just done a hard day's shoeing and didn't want to go out again, especially as I had just had rather a large meal, as befits a busy farrier. Anyway, I went.

On arrival, I was greeted by a young woman who appeared to be in charge of all things equine. She took me into a large tent where there were about twenty horses lined up in stalls. I thought, *Oh ma gawd*! and said to the lass, 'Which do you want shoeing?'

She replied, 'All of them; you can start here and shoe them all.'

Now, anyone who thinks that twenty horses can be shod between seven p.m. and bedtime doesn't seem to me to have much idea about horse shoeing, and as far as I was concerned, two were all she was getting done. So I said, 'Right, in that case I'd better get cracking.' And at that, she left me to it — thankfully.

They were all spotted stallions — Appaloosa type — and being entire, they grew feet a lot quicker than geldings or mares, and the first one I tackled was no exception. In fact the feet were so long that I doubt they had been trimmed for a very long time — like many months. Anyway, I gave them a good cutting back and refitted the old shoes. I had got a couple of the shoes nailed on, when I felt my neck being nuzzled, so I slapped at what I assumed to be another horse and said, 'Oi, put me down — you don't know where I've been!'

The lips kept slurping at the back of my neck, so I looked up and there was this great camel, with lips like a real up-to-date trout pout, licking and sucking at my neck, seemingly mistaking it for a salt lick. I was rather glad that I had almost finished that horse. Have you ever seen a camel's mouth at close range? It really is a sight to miss!

Anyway, I just shod one more and went to find the girl and told her that I had done them all. Not bad going, that: twenty horses in an hour and a half. Unfortunately, I only got paid for two. Ah, well, you can't win 'em all!

A Smelly Bath

A customer rang one day asking if I would go to his farm to dress some cows' feet; he said there were about a dozen (cows, that is, not feet). That could turn out to be quite a long job as well as being hectic and very dirty.

We made an arrangement for the visit in a few days' time. When the day arrived it was raining like you can't believe. The farmer said, 'It's all right, we've got them in the fold yard' – as if that would fill me with confidence! He had installed a cattle crush for the job, which had to make life a bit easier. Unfortunately, it was neither in nor out of the fold yard, but sort of half in and half out. Luckily, at least the opening end was just about under cover, and as that was the end where I would be required to work, there was half a chance of keeping dry. However, as with all fold yards, there was a large puddle of 'fold-yard gravy' running all the way down one side, not far from where the cattle crush was situated.

Whenever I did cows' feet, I always wore an old boiler suit, because you always end up covered all over in the brown smellies, and on this day it turned out to be a godsend. The farmer and his wife would drive a beast into the crush and fasten the head with the movable bar, and next we would rope a hind leg to a bar placed across the sides of the crush. Then I would get cracking with my hoof clippers and paring knife until something resembling the proper shape of a foot appeared. We then did the same to the other three feet and we finally released a smart-looking beastie back amongst its mates.

Things went along quite well apart from being lashed across the face by a filthy tail now and again, but we noticed that one particular beast wasn't going to wear being fastened in any cattle crush, and each time they tried to get that one in, it would just put its nose in and then duck out at the last second. We tried all ways, but it wasn't having any, so we decided to leave it till last.

We got all the others done and then it was the turn of the renegade once more. It wasn't very big, about three-quarters grown, so when it put its nose in the crush, I, daft as a brush, jumped forward and grabbed hold of its horns in an attempt to stop it from ducking out again. Well, it didn't like that either, and it gave an almighty heave, and I turned a somersault in the air, and landed on my back in the puddle of fold-yard gravy, which was about ankle deep! By the time I could pick myself up (unhurt, fortunately), my overall was soaking wet with this horrible-smelling liquid. I stripped it off sharpish and was quite relieved to see that my clothes underneath had kept fairly well clear of the evil-smelling stuff. We decided to leave that particular cow as she was.

The Hard Way

A former customer rang to say she had acquired a new pony for her young daughter and would I go and shoe it. When I arrived there, I saw that the new pony was a Welsh mountain pony — one of the light grey ones. The first thing the lady said — after the initial greeting, of course — was, 'Jane and I are going to hold it for you.'

Now, I have always had a deep-rooted suspicion of Welsh mountain ponies, because like a lot of small ponies, they are never properly broken in and they also tend to rear, and if you are holding on too tight, they can tip you on your face. Sometimes they will stand on one of your feet before rearing and it is then extremely difficult to dodge the flailing front hooves, and they don't care who they hit. So I said to the customer, 'Oh no you're not! I would rather tie it up and manage on my own.'

She said, 'But it's Jane's pony and she wants to hold it... don't you, Jane?'

Now Jane was about two years old, and didn't really care one way or the other — but I did. 'I really don't want Jane anywhere near,' I said. 'This is not the sort of job to involve young children in, as ponies don't care who they hurt if they decide to be funny.'

'Oh, all right then,' said the lady, clearly upset at having her plans scuppered, 'but *I* am going to hold it.'

'I can't stop you, if you insist,' I told her, 'but I wish you would change your mind, because I don't trust these small ponies as far as I can see them!'

Anyway, she insisted, and so that was that. I had tried.

I got all the feet dressed and all the new shoes fitted — not a muff. I then nailed the hind shoes on and clenched the nails up — not a muff. All this time my customer is leaning on the fence staring into space; it really is one of the most boring of jobs, standing holding a horse whilst it is being shod. I then lifted a front foot, pulled it between my knees and began to nail the new shoe on...

As soon as my hammer hit the first nail, the pony reared, its front feet going like pistons. It hit the dear lady in the middle of the forehead and she dropped like a sack of spuds under the fence. Well, I felt pretty bad about that, but I picked her up and carried her clear. As she came to, I asked if she was OK. She said that she was and asked what happened.

'Your pony thumped you,' I said.

'I didn't expect anything like that,' she said.

'No, but I thought it was a possibility, and I did try to warn you,' I said.

'Yes, well, you can manage on your own in future, and I'll be well out of the way.'

Lesson learned — the hard way.

Jasper — Influence

Jasper arrived at one of my livery yards and his name soon appeared on the shoeing list. He was a small pony, about 12.2, but he was a very strong, heavy-bodied animal. He was one of those that was all the same colour — a sort of dark chestnut, with a thick mane, tail and leg feathers. Plus, he had a bad temper. There was nothing he liked, except eating, and being out in the field. His owner could do nothing with him; he could only be ridden until he had had enough, and then he would throw the rider off and go back to the field.

Anyway, shoeing time came round, and he and I met for the first time. Well, he wasn't going to be shod, either; he made that very clear right from the off. So, I had to make it clear that he was, and boy, was there a battle! He sailed into me with hind feet, front feet and teeth, and even trapped me up against the stand side. I could hold onto his legs all day, but I needed two hands to do it, which meant I couldn't work. So I had no choice but to fight back. We proceeded to have a ding-dong battle, which I won enough to end up with shoes on. This procedure went on each time he was shod for quite a good few sets of shoes; he never came to accept that this was how life was going to be. It was always an unpleasant experience for both of us.

The yard owner asked me to judge the condition class at their annual show that year. The day duly arrived and there were about forty entries in the class. They were lined up in two long rows, with Jasper at the far end of the first row (I didn't know this, yet) and he was jumping about and generally making his owner's life a misery, as usual. I worked my way down the line until it was Jasper's turn to be judged. The owner told me this next bit. He said that Jasper had done nothing but misbehave all afternoon until I came to judge him. When I put my hand on his back and said, 'What's matter with you, then?' Jasper suddenly changed and became a different pony. He didn't put a foot wrong for the rest of the day. That's influence.

Strong Stuff

The telephone rang one night and a voice said, 'Is that the farrier?' I said something like, 'Aye, lad, who wants to know?'

The voice then said, 'My name is So-and-so and I have heard that you are good with bad horses.'

'Well you heard wrong,' says I. 'I am bad with bad horses.'

'Well, I have one that I would like you to have a go at,' he said. 'I've had three chaps to it already, and none have been able to get shoes on it.'

'OK,' I said, 'I'll see what I can do. But if it's as bad as you say, I might not be any more successful than the others, and I shall expect some sort of payment one way or the other.'

'That's fair enough,' he said. 'So will you come?'

So we made an arrangement for a visit.

When the day arrived, I got to the venue a good half-hour early. I must have got through my previous work in good time. The place was deserted, the only sign of life was a horse tied up in a mistal. *I wonder if this is it*, I thought. *There's one way to find out.* So I went up to the horse and said, 'Is it you, then?' The horse looked at me as if to say, 'Hello, another one here to see off.'

I ran my hand down its back and down its hind leg and said, 'Come on, then, let's see what you're made of.' As my hand reached its hock, it lashed out, but of course I was nowhere near the line of fire; I'd seen it all too often to get caught so easily. *This looks like it*, I thought, so off I went to see if there was anybody about.

I went and knocked on the house door but there was no reply, so I looked in the buildings and called out, but there didn't seem to be anyone here except me and the horse. I thought, *Right, I'll take a chance on this being the right one and make a start whilst it's quiet.* I got my toolbox out and my apron on and went in to the horse.

I have always started with the hind feet, a) because that's how we did it where I learned to shoe, and b) because I believe that if you crack 'em at the back first, by the time you get to the front where they can do most damage, they've generally got the idea. Down I went for the near hind and *bang*, it lashed out again, so I gave it a dose of 'Aunty Maggie's Remedy' – from an old George Formby song: it cured everything from ingrowing toenails to dandruff. Down I went again, and just the same thing happened, so I gave it another dose of AMR; but this time I said, 'Didn't you hear me first time?' I went down for the leg again and this time it came up a bit sharpish, but I was able to grab it firmly. 'That's more like it,' I said. 'Now just let's get on!'

I tapped round the foot with my buffer for a few seconds and talked quietly to the horse as I did so. I repeated the foot-tapping on all the feet, until I reckoned it was ready to accept the whole operation.

By the time the owner arrived, I had both hind shoes nailed on, and I was well on with a front shoe. When he saw the progress I had made his jaw dropped and he spluttered, 'How have you managed to get so far? The others couldn't get near it!'

I looked at him and with a dead straight face and said, 'It is the right horse, isn't it?'

'Well, yes,' he managed to say.

'Thank the Lord for that,' said I. 'I would hate to think I had shod the wrong one.'

'But how have you managed it?' he asked, amazed.

'A quick dose of "Aunty Maggie's Remedy",' I said, 'it works wonders.' He was still no wiser, and I didn't enlighten him.

I shod that horse for quite some time, and never had a moment's bother from it again; but the owner and his family could do nothing with it at all. I just used to tie it up and say, 'Come on, then, and just remember your manners,' and it behaved as if it had never known anything different. A dose of 'Aunty Maggie's Remedy' works wonders: powerful, strong stuff.

Perseverance

'Will you come and shoe my horse?' the voice on the telephone asked.

'Give me your phone number and address, and we'll call you as soon as my husband can do it,' said my wife, who dealt with all the telephone calls.

'It hasn't been shod before,' said the lady who owned the voice.

'I'll tell him,' said my wife, 'but all he'll say is, "So what? There's a first time for everything — we'll cross that bridge when we get to it." But at least he'll know.'

A few days later I arrived to shoe this horse and the first thing the lady said was, 'It hasn't been shod before.'

I said, 'Yes, my wife told me.'

'It's seven years old,' she said, 'and, er, it's a stallion.'

I never know what I am expected to do or say to that, as it's been said many times before. I think perhaps I should throw my hands in the air and shout, '*Mamma mia!*' or something. Instead I said, 'Well, I'm here now, so we may as well see what it's made of.'

I started to get my toolbox out and put my apron on, and the lady said, 'What would you like me to do?'

I answered, 'Well, if you'll put its head collar on and tie it up to that stake in the corner' — indicating a cow tie I had already spotted — 'I should be able to manage then, thank you.'

'I mean, what can I do to help?' she asked.

'The best thing you can do is go in the house and get on with whatever you would have been doing if I wasn't here,' I answered.

She looked at me for a moment then said, 'Will you be all right?'

'I hope so,' I said, 'but I'll give you a shout if I need anything.'

So, off she went, rather reluctantly, and I went into the stable to make a start.

It didn't want to have its legs picked up, and it made that clear right from the off. I thought, *Oh dear, it looks like being one of those jobs, does it*? So battle was joined. It didn't want shoeing, and I was going to shoe it. When I got a hind leg up, it pulled, heaved, jumped sideways and kicked out, but I stuck to its leg like a limpet and managed to get the foot dressed. I picked the other hind foot up, and that was no different; but, after a wrestling match, I completed the foot preparation on that one. So, to the front legs. Well, it pulled, pushed, and weighed down with all its might, trying to get its foot loose, but I was still there. By this time, my arms felt like they were being pulled from their sockets, as I had to fight for every move. The battle went on right to the bitter end, but I managed to get shoes on. I emerged from the stable feeling that I'd gone fifteen rounds with Henry Cooper.

'How did it go?' asked the owner as she saw me emerge from the stable.

'Well, it could have been a lot easier,' I said, 'but it should be better next time.'

Those turned out to be famous last words. It wasn't any easier next time, or the time after that, and I was getting fed up of being used as a punchbag by that horse…

When I next saw the lady's name in the diary for the fourth session, I said to my wife, 'This is the last time I go to that horse, if it's no better behaved this time.'

The stable where the horse was kept was at the top of a long, straight drive, and as you turned in off the road, you could see the horse's head hanging out of the stable door.

As I turned in that day, the first thing I saw was the head. As soon as the horse saw my van, it seemed to give an involuntary jerk, and the head promptly disappeared. I thought, *Aye, you b—, you know what's coming, don't you?*

I drove up, turned round and parked, jumped out and looked in the stable, and there was the horse standing in the corner, by the tethering stake, with no head collar on, with its nose touching the wall. I couldn't believe what I was seeing after the battles we had fought. I went in, put the head collar on, tied it up to the usual stake, and shod it without a murmur. I never had another minute's bother from that horse. It's a good job it didn't know that I, also, had had enough. That's perseverance.

The Garage Door

Many, many years ago, not all that long after I started my own business, I attended a horse at a nearby village. When I arrived there, the lady of the house came out and said that the horse belonged to her daughter, who was at school, and asked if I could manage on my own. I said that I would need to see what facilities there were first, and if there was anywhere suitable to tie the horse up, and if not, I would require someone to hold it. She said that she could not possibly hold it, as she was frightened to death by it. Anyway, we went to look. The stable in which the horse was kept was just big enough for the poor horse to turn round in – if it really tried – and there was no way on earth that I could shoe it in there.

We had a look round outside to see if there was anywhere suitable to tie the horse up. There were two alternatives: one was a telegraph pole, and the other was a garage door. The standing round the telegraph pole was very rough and stony, so the lady suggested tying the horse to the garage door – one of those with the handle in the middle. I said I would rather not do that, as it was not a very secure place. The lady said that if that was the best place for me to work, then she would take full responsibility for any mishap. As I have already mentioned, I was a bit green, and had never seen a horse pull back before. As soon as the rope was fastened, it sat back and pulled. The garage door parted company with the garage, flew over the horse's head and landed in the middle of its back with mighty thump. The horse gave a huge snort and set off down the yard, sort of crabwise, still firmly tied to the garage door. It managed to get to the middle of the field, then stood there snorting and trembling, and eyeing the garage door with apprehension… and guess who had to go and retrieve both horse and garage door — yeah, me!

As I approached the horse, it snorted some more and started backing off down the field, dragging the door after it. I managed to get to it and sweet-talk it into letting me attempt to loosen the rope, which of course had pulled tight, so I had to cut it. That left me without the means to tie it to the telegraph pole (I never did believe in giving in) — or did it? I remembered that I had just recently bought a nylon tow rope which had a loop in one end, so I made a makeshift halter out of it and thought, *Right, monkey, you won't break that!*

But boy, did it try! It laid back and pulled, shaking its head and really worrying that rope, but it held. I let the horse pull for a while until I was ready to start working on it. Fortunately, when I was actually holding the horse it behaved in a proper manner, and I was able to get on with shoeing it (and as that's all I had come for in the first place, all the bother was a bonus). But as soon as I let go, it started on the rope again. After all the excitement, I managed to finish the job, but it had been a real eye-opener for me. I heard later that the owner could do nothing else with the beast either, and it went back whence it came. I don't think anyone would miss it — I certainly didn't.

Eleven Months

I went to shoe a horse at a farm outside Leeds. The horse was the most beautiful palomino, very well set up, and with a big, bushy, flaxen mane and tail. There was no wonder it looked so good, as it was a stallion, and a very well-behaved stallion at that. It had quite large feet of a good, classic shape, and strong hooves of good quality dark-coloured horn. The horse was quite easy to shoe, and I got it done without difficulty.

'When will it need shoeing again?' asked the farmer.

'About six or eight weeks,' I answered.

'Right, I'll give you a ring,' said he.

When he finally called again, so much time had gone by that I had forgotten who he was, so I had to ask for directions. 'You've been before,' was the reply, as if that made things any different. Anyway, he still gave me the required directions, and by the time he had finished telling me, I began to remember.

When I arrived, the farmer said, 'Reight shoeing, that. They [the shoes] have been on eleven months – nivver seen owt like it!' – and neither had I. By this time I had clocked the feet, and couldn't believe what I was seeing. There was at least three inches of extra growth on them, and it looked as if the horse was standing on stilts. When I picked up a foot, there was what looked like a tiny shoe buried in this overgrown mass of horn, and as I have already written, the feet were naturally quite large; but with all the extra growth, they were grotesque.

It was something I had never encountered before, and I really felt sorry for such a good-looking animal to have such a thoughtless owner. To my mind, this sort of thing is abject cruelty. So I said to the owner, 'They won't stay on for eleven months this time.'

'How's that?' asked the owner.

'Because I'm not putting any shoes on, if this is how you are going to treat the poor bloody horse — it's disgusting.' And with that I took off all the shoes and gave the feet a birthday.

The owner didn't like it much, but tough. Perhaps he will be a bit more considerate in future, but I doubt it. Over the years since this episode, I have come to the conclusion that some farmers are very inconsiderate towards the welfare of their animals. Anyway, I went away with a clear conscience, knowing that I had done the horse a favour.

Hot Toddy

I was called to a place to shoe a horse and trim a donkey's feet one winter's day. The weather was atrocious, with snow blowing horizontally in the wind. It was one of those places where there is no shelter, and when the ground was soft, I couldn't drive up to the stable block, so I had to manage out in the fresh air, get cold and wet, or go away unpaid. As I'm not in the habit of doing that, I got a jumper on and an almost waterproof jacket, and got stuck in.

The mare in question had never been one of the easiest of animals to deal with, and what with the weather an' all, I looked like being in for a bit of a rough ride. I had got fairly well on with the shoeing, when a voice called out, 'Would you like a drink?'

It was the master of the household. Thinking he meant tea or coffee, I called back, 'Yes, please,' and continued with my work.

A short while later the chap appeared with a glass tumbler full of steaming golden liquid. He said, 'Get that down you, it'll warm you up no end.'

It was whisky and hot water — a tumbler full. By the time I had got that down, everything suddenly seemed better: the snow wasn't as cold and wet, the mare was better behaved, and I wasn't sure whether the birds were singing or not.

Anyway, I got my job completed, and I must have got the shoes on the right way round (nobody ever said), and started on the donkey. I had just made a start, when out came the owner with another golden tumblerful.

'I thought you could perhaps use another one,' he said.

Well, one thing my father always said was, 'Never refuse an offer, you may never get another.' So I set to work on both donkey and hot toddy. It was a good job that it was dinnertime soon after, so I could get some blotting paper — in the form of sandwiches — down me, and I'm sure I swallowed them whole. I came round somewhat after something to eat, and a bit of a rest, and managed to finish my day's work without too much hardship. But I found out that day that horse shoeing and booze do not mix very well, and are best undertaken separately.

Hard Faced

Many years ago, one of my customers decided to ride her horse from Land's End to John o' Groats and back, in aid of 'Riding for the Disabled'. She spent two years or so in the planning and preparation, and she asked me, as her farrier, to experiment with various hardening devices so that her horse could cope with the roadwork involved.

The horse was an Arabian stallion and its feet were quite small, but it wore the outside branches of the hind shoes very badly indeed. I asked the owner to first do a check on the miles she rode in training, so that we had a starting point. As I remember, it did about a hundred miles on ordinary shoes, but that wasn't much use, as the horse would do that in four days when she got under way. Ideally, it needed to be able to do nearer six hundred miles on one set of shoes, or it would need shoeing once a week; and that was no good for either horse or owner.

The next time I shod it, I made an extra set of shoes which were sent for case-hardening. I was not confident that this would be much good, because it only puts a very thin skin of hardness on, which would soon be scrubbed off. In the event I was right; it was unsuccessful, as it only added a few miles to the original hundred, so we were back to square one.

Deep in my memory I remembered some stuff (I like that word — it covers endless ground) called 'Stellite', and although I had never actually used it, I knew that it had the sort of properties that we were looking for. I went to the welding suppliers and bought a few rods to try. It had to be sort of sweated on, using oxyacetylene welding gear which I always carried anyway. I started off with a blob just behind the outside toe, as this was the prime wearing area, and straight away there was a marked improvement. The owner and I had a powwow and decided that a blob twice as big at the toe and a smaller one at the outside heel should just about do the business. With this method, the horse managed to do just over the six hundred miles mark in training, so we decided that that should be enough.

At the last shoeing before the off, I made four spare sets of shoes, all liberally dosed with Stellite, so they could stop at a shoeing shop and just get the shoes changed, and I agreed to meet them at Preston on the way south, and do a full job on the feet.

The first set of shoes lasted to John o' Groats, the second set lasted back to Preston, the third set got them to Land's End, and the fourth set got them home: now that's what I call hard faced! I don't think we could have done much better than that without making the shoes from Stellite altogether, which was an impossibility, and the owner was quite pleased. And I bet she still has that other spare set.

The Horse That Could Count

Many years ago, I used to shoe a horse that I came to believe could count – up to five anyway. It was an ordinary riding pony, about 14.2 and a bit of a cob type. It was generally quite good to shoe, but it had this bad habit of rearing when I was nailing the near foreshoe on. What made it remarkable was the fact that it always reared when I was driving the fifth nail in. I had shod it quite a few times before I realised this fact, maybe five or six times, when I suddenly remembered that it was always the same nail, in the same hole. It was also the only time it reared; once I was passed that particular nail, there was no more trouble.

I should explain here that I always nailed the shoes on in the same sequence, so that the shoe did not move. I always started with the second hole from the toe on the right of the shoe as, being right-handed, I could hold the shoe in place quite easily, without hitting my fingers, and without the shoe trying to twist round so much. Next I would put the opposite nail in, the second toe hole on the left side, next would be the right side toenail (or the hole nearest the toe), then the left side toenail. The third nail on the right would follow, then the third on the left, followed by the outside heel nail, whichever side that happened to be on. The reason why I have explained all this rigmarole is important to the tale as you will see.

I would get the first, second, third and fourth nails in without any difficulty, but as soon as I tried the fifth nail, the horse would rear. This can be quite dangerous, as there are already four sharp nails sticking out of the side of the hoof, and, if you make a grab for it, you can easily end up with four pieces missing out of your finger ends.

By the time I had realised that it was always the same nail, I thought, a bit tongue-in-cheek, *This bloody horse can count! Let's see if I can bamboozle it.* So, daft as a brush, I started with the same first two nails in my sequence, and then I put in what should have been the fifth nail, then followed with the rest. You wouldn't believe it, but the horse did not rear, even when the fifth nail went in, albeit in a different hole. I still don't know why it didn't rear, but I used this sequence of nailing on each time after that, and I never had any more trouble. I am still convinced that that horse could count − whether it could or not, it was quite uncanny.

A Cuddly Shetland Pony

I was called to a place to trim the feet of a Shetland pony that I had not seen before. Despite what most people think about cuddly Shetlands, this can be a very difficult task, and you must go prepared for anything. I always made sure I had my own head collar, because many Shetland pony owners never seem to catch them, and when they do, a piece of clothes line or some such is all they seem to use. The next essential piece of equipment is a pair of steel toe-capped boots, as Shetlands are very good at standing on your toe with a hind foot, then, when you are well and truly trapped, they will rear and come at you with front feet flailing, and there is no way out. The steel toecaps don't help you to get out, but they do help to protect your toes. The next essential is to find a good tying-up place, because they can get away from four men much easier than a gatepost.

So, duly prepared, I arrived at the farm where the pony was kept, and was most disconcerted to see that the pony had access to five fields. I thought, *This looks like being one of those jobs*, as, with all that grass to go at, it was bound to be overfed, and there is nothing worse than an overfed Shetland pony. I had arrived a few minutes before the owner, and was looking round for a good tying-up place when he arrived.

'What are you looking for?' he asked.

'Somewhere to tie the pony up,' I replied.

'It's reight,' he said, 'I'll hod it.'

'I don't think you will,' I said, 'it could be a bit awkward.'

'What, that?' he asked.

'Aye, that,' I replied, 'I think it would be better tied up.'

'What's up wi' yer?' he asked. 'I'll hod it, don't thee bother.'

'Well, I did warn you, and we'll soon find out,' I said.

So we got started — in the corner of the laithe porch. I had no sooner lifted a leg, than there was a scuffle, and the owner and pony were in a heap on the ground. 'What are you doing down there?' I asked with a straight face.

'It took me by surprise,' he said, picking himself up after the pony had scrambled to its feet.

'Are you ready this time?' I asked him.

'I'm ready,' he replied, so down I went for the foot again. Immediately there was another scuffle, and there they were in a heap on the ground again.

'I thought you were ready,' quoth I.

'Well, er…' he managed to say… 'I'm ready this time,' he concluded, so down I went for the foot. Scuffle, in a heap on the ground again.

'Don't you think I should find that tying-up place now?' I said.

'Aye, 'appen tha'd better,' he said. 'I didn't think it would be like that.'

'Well, I did warn you,' I said.

So I tied it to a gatepost and it tried to get away as before, but of course, the gatepost wouldn't give in — but oh! how the pony tried. After a while, when it decided that it couldn't get away, it quietened down enough for me to get the job done. The owner decided that he didn't need a Shetland pony any more, and got shut of it.

Excuses

I once got a call from a chap who asked if I would trim a few donkeys' feet. When I asked how many (donkeys), he said there would be about nine or ten. It seemed a bit strange to me that the chap didn't know whether he had nine or ten donkeys to do, but ours is not to reason why. Anyway, I said I would go. I wondered how much time to allow to trim the feet of ten donkeys, as you can bet your sweet life that at least some of them would be a bit difficult. I decided to allow four hours — all morning — so I called the customer and said I would be there at eight o'clock the following morning, if that was OK. He said yes, it was OK, so I duly presented myself at his farm at the agreed eight o'clock the following morning, complete with my own head collar, rope and steel toe-capped boots. These items are essential when working on donkeys and Shetland ponies, because many owners don't have their own head collars or ropes, and quite often, I have had to make do with a piece of clothes line, or baling string. The steel toecaps are vital for survival — as I have already stated.

Well, eight o'clock came, but no one arrived, so I waited... and waited... and waited... and still nobody arrived. I had to ask myself how long I thought was reasonable to wait, as I had to have that job completed by about twelve o'clock, because I had booked other work. I told myself, 'Right, nine o'clock is the deadline, if nobody turns up by then, I will have to go.' So, nine o'clock came — and went — and nobody appeared, so I started up my van, and was just about to drive off, when a car came swishing into the yard. A chap jumped out and came over to the van and said, 'Are you leaving?'

I said, 'Yes, I can't stay any longer, as there are other customers to go to, and we haven't even got a start yet. By the time you have caught the donkeys it will be far too late.'

'I'm sorry I am so late,' he said, 'I've just got out of jail.'

Well, there's no answer to that, is there?

Staggered

I received a call one day from a woman asking me to go and shoe her show stallion; she said it needed its feet doing badly, because it was being put down. At the time, I thought she meant shot, and I couldn't understand why she needed its feet tidy for that. It turned out that she meant it was being moved down the line in the show ring because its feet were too long. When I got there, I found it was a Welsh Section A stallion, and it was fat. I can never understand why people in the showing world must have their horses so fat that they can hardly waddle. It always seemed to me that they took a perfectly reasonable animal, stuffed it with oats, and then called it a show horse.

Anyway, there I was with this pony, and the job had to be done. It wasn't keen on being shod, as I expected from its size, but I managed to get the hind feet trimmed without too much trouble. When it came to the front feet, however, it was a vastly different tale. As soon as I tried to lift one, it reared, front feet going like pistons – and how do you shoe feet that are two yards off the ground and moving like greased lightning? Well, I had had experience of these little bleeders before, and I thought, *I know what you need, matey*!

I loosened the tying-up rope, with difficulty, as it had been pulled tight with the rearing, then re-tied it using a slack, quick release knot, and as I asked it for a front foot again, I kept the loose end in my hand. As soon as the pony reared, I pulled the rope to undo the knot. The pony had expected to hit the end of the rope as usual, and got the surprise of its life when there was no rope there, and it began staggering backwards in an effort to regain its balance.

It staggered right across the building — about ten yards or so — before losing the battle for balance, then fell over on its back against the wall. I followed it across the building and thumped it until it got up, and said, 'What do you think about rearing now, then?'

I led the pony back to the tying-up place and re-tied it using the quick release knot again. As soon as I asked for the foot, it did its circus act again, and once more I thumped it until it got up. After the second time, it must have seen the light, because it suddenly seemed to lose interest in rearing.

If only owners would spend time teaching their animals how to behave, there would be no need for this sort of caper; but whenever I complained, all the reply I got — and from different owners — was, 'Well, it is a stallion, what do you expect?'

Well, I for one expect the animals to know how to behave.

Child Psychology

It was nine o'clock in the morning and I had just arrived at my customers' home to shoe their pony called Sally. Sally was a Welsh Section A Arabian cross, making it about 14 hands high and the usual light grey colour. Sally didn't get ridden very much and could be a bit silly at times, but she seemed to be in good spirits this morning. I opened up my trailer and got my toolbox out containing my hand tools, and took out my protective apron, which I proceeded to buckle round my waist. With the leg straps fastened, I was ready to get on with the actual operation of shoeing Sally.

The shoeing operation is in four parts. The first part is to remove the old shoes and trim the feet, the second part is to shape and fit the new shoes, the third part is to nail the new shoes onto the feet, and the final part is to clench the nails and rasp off. I got as far as dressing the first foot, when the young child of my customer appeared riding in a toy car. It rattled on the concrete surface of the yard, making such a racket that poor old Sally began to peep round and fidget. At first it was just a bit of restlessness, but as the child got nearer to Sally she became really upset, so much so that she was becoming difficult to work on. At this point I said to my customer, 'Will you please ask the child to stop riding in the car until I have finished, as Sally is becoming quite restless?'

So Mother said to the child, 'Darling, will you please stop riding in your car until the farrier has finished shoeing Sally, as she is becoming frightened.'

The child continued to clatter round the yard as if Mother had not spoken.

By this time, poor old Sally had started to tremble with anxiety and I knew from past experience that the next move from old Sally would be evasive action. This usually consists of jumping violently in an attempt to escape from the source of trouble. This can lead to the farrier getting some sort of injury, and I don't see why I should take any more injuries than I can help; so I said to my customer once more, 'Will you *please* ask the child to leave the toy until I have finished?'

So the dear lady said to the child, '*Please*, darling, will you put the car away?'

So the child kept on clattering round as though Mother had not spoken. The situation was by now becoming quite desperate as far as I was concerned, so I put on my finest glower and said to the child:

'*GerroffthatbikenowandIwon'ttellyoutwice!*'

Weeell, there was a deathly hush for a second or two, and then the child jumped off the toy and ran to Mummy with a resounding '*WHAAAaaaaaa!*' Fortunately for me, Sally seemed to understand '*WHAAAaaaaaa*', for she calmed down straight away as soon as the rattling stopped. I said to my customer, 'That's how to do it.'

She said, 'Yes — so it seems.'

Unfortunately I only got paid for the shoeing, and not for the lesson in child psychology.

Hand Reared

A very good, long-standing customer bought a new hunter and needed it shoeing. When I arrived, the groom had it already tied up in a freshly cleaned out box — ah, what luxury! The animal was a very nice-looking black mare, with white socks, about sixteen hands and a good build, which, when fully fit, should be able to hunt all day.

The groom was standing at its head, which I thought a bit odd, as he usually gets things ready and then leaves me to it. Anyway, I got my toolbox out and apron on, and went into the box to make a start. I put my box down in position, and ran my hand down a hind leg (I always started at the back) to ask for a foot... well, I got two. The mare let out a blood-curdling scream, and lashed out with both hind feet, and I had to jump for my life. It screamed and lashed out three times in very quick succession, in fact until I had managed to scramble out of the door. It didn't just lash out any old how, it followed me round until I was out of the box. I considered myself quite fortunate not to have had any help with my rather undignified exit. I said to the groom, 'What's going on here? That was a bloody close call.'

He said he thought it had stopped doing that since it arrived, as it had done the same to him in the first place, but he had worked at it and it seemed OK.

So that's why he was standing at its head, is it? I asked myself. I said, 'It's OK, now I know how the cookie crumbles, I'll have another go.'

So in I went, daft as a brush, and the same thing happened again — there was this horrible scream, and *bang-bang-bang* again until I was out of the door.

The groom said, 'I can lift its feet up and it doesn't bother. I'll lift one up and you come in behind me and take over.'

He got a foot up without any bother, and gave it a bit of a tapping, so I went in behind him, as in plan 'B', but as soon as I touched it, we both had to jump for our lives. I said, 'I'm not going to get shoes on that today, as it's not easy nailing shoes on feet that are flying past your ear! You will have to give it a good lunging for a few days to wear it out, and I'll come back later in the week and try again.'

The next time I went, as soon as I touched it, it just lashed out, sort of half-heartedly, with no squealing this time, and I managed to grab the foot as it whizzed past. Carefully, I tapped its foot to see what sort of reaction I could expect when I started shoeing. To my surprise, it didn't mind, and I was able to shoe it quite easily. As it was ridden more, it became even more amenable, until one day it received an injury whilst out hunting, which required it to be turned out and not used for several weeks.

When it was ready to return to work and needed shoes on again, it was back to screaming and lashing out again. Fortunately — or unfortunately, depending on your point of view — its intended victim was the owner. He escaped by the skin of his teeth, but it shook him up a bit, so he decided to get rid of it. Nobody argued; in fact the groom and I breathed a mutual sigh of relief.

It transpired that the mare's mother had died giving birth to it, and it had been hand reared by the then owner, and it didn't recognise horses as its own kind, and wanted to associate with humans all the time. I don't know whether that had any bearing on its behaviour or not, but it was the strangest sort of situation I had ever come across — and I don't want to come across another. A vet once told me that this sort of behaviour was something to do with the ovaries, but I think it had something to do with what's between the ears.

The groom also told me of another situation concerning this mare during the time it was turned out through injury.

He was going about his business one day when he heard a faint voice calling, 'Help, help.' He looked around and couldn't see anything amiss, but still the voice came: 'Help.' So he set off to investigate, and found a telephone linesman up a pole in the field where this mare was running out. The mare was at the foot of the pole looking up at the linesman − presumably looking for human companionship − and the poor chap was frightened to death to come down; I must say, I don't blame him, after the reception she gave me when we first met. Anyway, the groom rescued the poor chap, who probably never trusted horses again − and rightly so!

A Thorn in the Flesh

I shod for a small hunting yard for many years. The owners were very fastidious, and looked after their animals well, so I used to go there quite regularly to keep them well shod. At the time I am writing about, the husband was still working, so I used to make their yard my first stop of the day. I would arrive there at eight o'clock in the morning, and he would tell me which horses needed my attention, make sure I had all I needed, and then he would go in the house for breakfast before setting out for work.

On this particular morning, he told me that his big mare wasn't quite sound, and said that he couldn't find anything wrong with it, and asked me to have a good look round to see if I could find anything. The first thing to do with any lameness is to find out which leg the horse is lame on. Accordingly, I asked the owner to trot it up so I could be sure where to look, and also see just how bad the lameness was. I identified the offending limb after only a few steps, and the mare was 'nodding' quite badly, so there was obviously something there that needed finding. The owner left me to get on whilst he went and got himself ready for work, and I took the shoe off the lame limb, cleaned the foot, and trimmed it ready to take a new shoe. By doing this, a nice clean foot surface is exposed, and it is much easier to see any telltale black marks, which may identify a puncture wound, but there were none. I thought, *This looks like being a bit difficult, and it looks like I am going to have to sing for my supper* — meaning that I was going to have to work hard to find the trouble.

I gently scraped away at the surface of the sole, hoping to find a mark of some sort: nothing. So I started to clean up the heels, when I thought I felt the loop of my knife snag on something. 'Ah, bingo!' I said, probably out loud, and carefully scraped round the area to identify the source of the snag. When I found it I couldn't believe what I was seeing. There was what looked like the branch of a tree buried right in the corner where the hoof wall bends back to form the bar. The piece was about half an inch in diameter, and I had no way of knowing how far in it had gone, so I went to the house and said to the owner, 'You had better come and look at this before I go any further.'

'Have you found something?' the owner asked.

'You could say that,' I replied, 'and I want you to see it before I touch it again, *and* I want you to be there when I remove the problem.'

'Sounds serious,' he said.

'Well, we'll soon find out,' was my reply.

I searched round in the lockers of my trailer, and found two sharp objects which I hoped would pierce the piece of wood from each side, and so enable me to lever it out. I also got a wad of cotton wool to mop up any blood. The piece of wood came out with a nice 'slurp', and it was about an inch long, and had gone straight in, fortunately causing no damage to the pedal bone, and there was not even much blood.

Anyway, I cleaned it up with some peroxide to be on the safe side, and my customer went off to work a bit happier than he might have done. By the time I had put a new shoe on the foot, the horse was totally sound. It's nice to win one as easy as that.

Thick!

I used to attend this particular customer at least once a fortnight, so I looked upon him as a very good customer. I went on this occasion to shoe a new pony he had bought for his daughter. The pony looked to be an Arab-Welsh cross, about thirteen hands high, greyish, and altogether a nice-looking animal — that is, until you looked at its feet.

Normal feet of a pony this size would be roughly 2½" high at the middle of the side on the slope, but these feet were about six inches high, with a shoe perched on the end. Fortunately for the pony, the feet had grown straight down, with no 'turn-in', 'turn-out' or 'turn-up' to cause any added problems.

Well, I looked at these feet and wondered which window cleaner had shod them, and more importantly, what I would be able to do about them, as I had never seen anything like this in my entire career — and I have never seen anything like them since, thankfully. I said to my customer, 'These are about ready for a trim, aren't they?' and he replied, 'Yes, aren't they a funny shape?'

I replied, 'Aye, at least that.'

So, I set to and took the first shoe off, and the hoof was just a solid mass, the wall and sole was one big, thick lump, and it was so hard that my hoof nippers would not cut it. I took the other shoes off, and the hooves were all the same, hard as rocks and un-cuttable. I told the owner the problem, and suggested that I leave the feet un-shod this time, and I would look at them again on my next visit, which could be no more than two weeks away. He said, 'If that's what you think best, OK, do that.' I told him that if his daughter had been riding the pony up until now, there was no reason why she shouldn't continue to ride it, as riding it was unlikely to do the feet any harm; in fact, it might even do them a bit of good.

On my next visit, which was only the following week, as it happened, I got the main work done, and then asked about the new pony.

'Oh, it's been fine,' said the owner, and went on to say that his daughter had been riding it, and it seemed to be going a bit better than it had been before.

When I saw it, the feet still looked the same length as they had done on my previous visit, but when I picked one up, it was like looking down a short length of 3½" diameter tube. The excess sole had disappeared and left only the wall, which was still about a good three inches too long. This was fairly easily removed, and suddenly the hooves were back to a normal shape — just as if they had never been any different. So I put a set of shoes on, and bingo, problem solved.

I have often wondered since, how anybody who knows anything about horse shoeing could do a job like that. They are certainly not fit people to be caring for animals. I couldn't make my mind up which was thickest, the feet or the farrier...

A Good Doer

This tale concerns a customer whose horse was a huge animal with a large barrel body. The lady owner was a keen hunter who hunted three days a week. The horse carried her quite easily and she had no difficulty getting through the hunting season. At the end of the season, the horse was turned away for the summer, as is the usual practice with hunting horses, and I went and trimmed its feet a couple of times during the summer. I mentioned to the lady that I thought the horse was getting a bit fat, and advised her to be a bit careful.

Anyway, the time came for the horse to be brought in to get it fit for the hunting season, and I duly went and shod it up ready, again commenting on its weight. She started working it, and noticed that it was pottering a bit at the front, so she rang me to ask if I was sure that I had not nail-bound it. I said that I was sure, but would come and check it out all the same. I examined each foot carefully, and could find nothing wrong, so I told her that I thought that the horse needed a lot of weight off with diet and exercise, and it would gradually become sound again.

She rang me a few days later, and said that she had had her vet look at it, and he said that it had navicular disease, and would I go and shoe it accordingly. I said that I would, if she insisted, but I had already told her what I thought about it, and I reckoned she would be wasting my time and her money to no advantage. I repeated what I had told her about its weight, and she said that she would think about it for a while. Well, she called me again a few days later to say that she had had a second opinion, and this time the horse had a shoulder injury, and asked what I thought about that. I asked why she was asking my opinion again, when I had already given it twice, and that if she wanted me to come and do something, just tell me what she had decided, and I would come and see to it.

I didn't hear from her for a further few weeks, until her shoeing time was up, and she called me to go and shoe the horse again. I asked her how it was, and she said that she had sent it to the veterinary place at Liverpool, to see if they could sort it for her. They had kept it there for a couple of weeks, and done all the tests on it, and could find nothing wrong; so they suggested that she reduce its weight with diet and exercise, and it should come sound gradually. And it did. I resisted the urge to say 'I told you so', but she did admit that if she had taken my advice in the first place, the horse would have been sound a darned sight quicker and at a lot less cost. We live and learn.

Away in a Manger

The first time I went to this particular customer to shoe her horse, she had a young baby with her, probably about three months old or so. The stable was quite small – in fact, not much bigger than the horse – and there was no pram or pushchair to be seen; so I wondered what the lady planned to do with the baby while she held the horse during shoeing, as there didn't look to be a tying-up place. I soon found out. She spread a blanket on the hay in the manger, and laid the baby on that while she stood next to it holding the horse. The baby was quite snug there and safely out of harm's way.

As I have already mentioned, the stable was very small, and the horse quite large, so that when I was working on the hind feet, I had to stand with one foot outside and down a step, and the other foot inside on top of the step. (Sometimes the facilities in the shoeing job are quite enviable.) This made the job quite difficult, but I could not stand with both feet outside, because if the horse had pulled for any reason, I would have been unable to move my feet, and would have ended up in a heap under the horse, which is not a very healthy place to be. Fortunately, the horse was pretty good to do, and I shod it like that many times.

Meanwhile, the baby grew, and was soon taking notice of things. On one visit he (yes, it was a boy) was being carried by his mother, and I went up to him with my fists raised, and said, 'Can ta feight?' ('Can you fight' – for the uninitiated.) Well, the poor lad let out a yell, and started crying as if the world was about to end. I apologised profusely to his mother, as I hadn't meant to frighten the poor lad.

'Oh, he'll get over it,' she said, 'don't bother about it.' Unfortunately, every time the little lad saw me for ages after that, he would run to his mother and start crying.

Anyway, time went by, and the little lad started school, and I didn't see much of him after that, and I forgot all about the incident.

One day, many years later, this tall young chap came into the yard as I was doing some shoeing for his mother, who by now had bought a small farm and was doing liveries, and I heard the word 'Mother'. So, after he'd gone, I asked my customer who the young man was.

'Don't you remember him?' she said. 'That's the baby you frightened half to death that day!' She then went on to tell me that she used to use me as the bogeyman, and whenever she was having difficulty with him she would say, 'Now behave yourself, or I'll tell the blacksmith!' — and that would usually do the trick. The lad grew to be about six feet tall, and did some weight training, so I never repeated the question; and anyway, he had already forgiven me — I think!

Stampede

I had finished shoeing a horse for a customer one particular day, down at the bottom of a long, narrow farm road. I was just setting off to my next appointment when I noticed a herd of cattle coming down the lane. There were at least twenty of them, and at the front was a big Limousin bull. They filled the lane from side to side and were coming at a good trot. The farmer's wife was standing in the middle of the lane outside the farmyard entrance. I stopped by her and asked where the cattle were going, as I had no chance of getting out of the way.

'I'm going to turn them into the yard,' she said confidently, so I volunteered to park across the lane to help turn them into the yard. She was standing in front of my 4x4 and trailer, and I stayed in the driving seat, as I didn't think there would be any need for me to help. But them beasties were getting nearer, and were coming at such a rate of knots, that I said to the lady, 'These b—s aren't going to turn, they're coming too fast!'

When it became obvious that the cattle were not going to turn, the lady suddenly disappeared − where to, I never found out, as I was busy worrying about the health of my car, which was quite obviously going to catch a mauling. The huge bull tried to put the brakes on, but the pressure of the herd behind him and the other front-runners was so great that they had no chance of either stopping or turning into the yard. My vehicle was almost completely blocking the lane, and the bull decided that the only way out was to go over my car bonnet.

So that's what he tried to do. He failed quite miserably, and landed across the bonnet, staring me in the face through the windscreen, while he tried to scramble off. Meanwhile the rest of the herd either tried to follow the bull, or scramble through what little gap there was between car and wall. My car needed a new bonnet and wing, but considering what the tonnage of beef was that had passed over it, round it and almost through it, I thought that I had got off quite lightly.

Fortunately, the farmer was insured, and had no hesitation in claiming responsibility; and even more fortunately, his wife suddenly re-appeared — unharmed. I never found out where she had gone to avoid injury, or where the cattle ended up, and I didn't stop to find out. I might not have been so fortunate if they had returned.

Selective Memory

A long-established customer of mine bought a new jumping pony, and asked me to go and shoe it. It was about 13.2 and a BSJA-registered showjumper. The first thing I noticed about it was its feet (well, surprise, surprise, it's the first thing I notice about any horse). They were a very bad shape, long at the toe, low at the heel and far too thick — in fact everything they should not be. It also had toe-clipped, rolled toe shoes on the hind feet, and I must say I thought it had been shod by the postman, or perhaps the window cleaner; certainly not by a farrier who knew what he was about.

I said to the owner, 'It's certainly about ready for its feet doing.'

'It's come from So-and-so's yard' — mentioning the name of a well-known rider on the showjumping circuit — 'and he said it has to be shod like this or it overreaches and pulls shoes off.'

'That's hardly surprising,' I said. 'I'm only surprised it can even walk about, never mind jump fences with feet like that! But when I've finished with it, it will neither over-reach nor pull shoes off again, and it *won't* be shod like that.'

'But So-and-so says it's *got* to be shod like that,' my customer retorted, getting a bit miffed that I was questioning the opinion of So-and-so.

I said, 'Look, its feet are all wrong, and I don't care who says otherwise, and I don't even *know* how to shoe that badly.'

'But So-and-so said—'

'I'll tell you what I'll do,' I said, cutting him short, 'I'll shoe the pony my way, and if it overreaches or pulls a shoe off within eight weeks, I'll come and shoe it again for free. Now I can't say fairer than that, can I?'

At this point I must tell you that this customer was one of my least fastidious owners when it came to looking after his horses' feet. Three months was a minimum time for him to go between visits, but this will be the subject of my next story.

Anyway – to continue. He reluctantly agreed to my offer, and I duly set about making it good, with feet nicely dressed and balanced, and quarter clips on the hind shoes. It was probably about three months before I went to this pony again, and it still had four shoes on, and no overreach marks. I said to the owner, 'How's the overreaching then?'

He looked at me a bit funny and said, '*That* pony has never overreached.' He had obviously forgotten all about So-and-so and what *must* be done.

I didn't say anything to that, but just licked my thumb and made a couple of stripes down the front of my shirt. A case of selective memory if ever I saw one.

The Horse That's Always Losing Shoes

In my last story, 'Selective Memory', I mentioned that the owner in that tale was not very fastidious when it came to looking after his horses' feet. Well, here's the story behind that comment.

He bought a big showjumping horse for his daughter, and asked me to shoe it for him. It had quite big feet with good quality horn, and was reasonably good to do, and I didn't expect any problems — like lost shoes or overreaches — and after finishing the job, I left feeling quite satisfied that all would be OK. As usual when I finished a job, I promptly forgot all about it, knowing that if there was a problem, I would hear about it soon enough.

Some time later, the owner rang to say that the horse had lost a shoe, and was jumping at the weekend (as they do). I thought nothing about it at the time, because I knew it had been some weeks since I had shod it, and I called and re-shod it on my rounds — before the weekend.

At this place I was always left alone to get on, and, if a horse was reasonable to deal with, I much preferred to be alone, as I could carry out my work without stopping to talk. In this case, being alone meant that I could not mention the length of the feet to the owner until I had finished the job, by which time I had forgotten anyway. Again I went away and forgot about it.

The next time I was called to this horse, the owner again referred to it as 'the one that's always losing shoes', and said that they were jumping at the weekend (again); so I told him that at least he got his money's worth out of them first, as it had been quite some time since it had been shod. Once

65

more I thought no more about it, until he rang the next time, and 'the one that's always losing shoes' had lost another – and, yes, they were jumping at the weekend.

By this time I was beginning to take notice, and I thought it was about time I looked up just how long the shoes were actually staying on between shoeings. So I checked back, right to the beginning when I first started shoeing that horse for him. The average length of time between visits was fourteen weeks, so I told the owner that he was only supposed to go six to eight weeks, and if he did that, the horse was unlikely to ever lose another shoe. Needless to say, he didn't believe that he was going so long between shoeings, and was convinced that shoes were being chucked off right, left and centre.

So, being a fair-minded man, I said I would do a deal with him. I offered to call every ten weeks and re-shoe the horse, and I guaranteed that it would not lose another shoe. Reluctantly, he agreed, and it lost no more shoes. However, even after the horse was retired from jumping, he still referred to it as 'the horse that was always losing shoes'. Sometimes, you just can't win.

Lice

Maybe this is not the best of subjects to include in a series of stories, but on several occasions I have been inundated with these unpleasant creatures. I would get the odd one on my arm quite regularly, but on occasions the number of lice has been quite disgusting.

I once went to a farm to shoe two horses; they had been running out all winter with sheets on. When the owner removed the sheets for me to shoe the horses, there were lice hanging off them like bunches of grapes — they were absolutely crawling. It looked to me like the sheets had not been removed all winter. I thought that I had seen most things in my time, but this was something totally unexpected, and it turned my stomach, and I almost refused to work on them. However, I had travelled a long way to do this job, and I reflected that going away and leaving them was going to leave a rather large hole in my income for that day.

So I set to, and got the horses shod, and gave myself as good a brush off as I could before leaving. Fortunately, I was going straight home after this job, so I would not be spreading lice all over Yorkshire. People say that lice don't live long on humans, but when I arrived home, I rolled my sleeves down before going in the house, and found that the sleeve turn-ups were crawling with lice. I took my shirt off there and then, and threw it in the dustbin. When I went in the house, my wife asked what had happened to my shirt, and I told her it was in the best place it could possibly be.

I went to another place, at another time, to trim some ponies' feet. It was rather a posh place where they bred pedigree Dartmoor ponies. There were about twenty of them to trim, and I arrived there at eight o'clock in the morning to do the job. I had got a couple or so done, when I felt the familiar tickle on my arm, and there was a louse crawling up my arm. I flicked it off, and I said to the owner, 'Your pony has lice.'

'Oh, you didn't get those here,' she said in her very posh voice.

'Well, I didn't bring them with me at eight o'clock in the morning, either,' was my reply.

I used to see quite a lot of this sort of thing, particularly in the spring, when the animals had been running out with sheets on — out of sight, out of mind, is the phrase that springs to mind.

The Coffee

I first met the lady of this story at a riding school that I used to attend every week, where her young daughter was having riding lessons. Although I never had occasion to talk to her, she always seemed to me to be a very nice woman, always immaculately dressed, immaculately groomed and very precisely spoken.

One day I received a telephone call from a new customer, to go to their home and shoe a newly acquired pony. When I arrived at the house, I was met by this same lady, and it seemed that she had bought a pony for the young daughter.

The pony was only quite young, and not very well behaved, and wasn't very keen on being tied up to be shod. In fact, it wasn't very keen on anything, and showed its displeasure by pulling back as soon as it was tied up. There was only me and the lady of the house about, so I asked her to stand with the pony whilst I tried to get on with the job of getting some shoes on it. She wasn't very keen on that idea, but she stood with it anyway and I managed to get the job done. As soon as I had finished, she heaved a sigh of relief, and asked if I would like a cup of coffee. I said yes, I would, so off she went into the house to put the kettle on. She was soon back with the steaming brew, and it was the best coffee I have ever tasted; I thanked her and commented on how nice the coffee was, and then I went away and forgot all about it — as you do as soon as you are faced with the next equine challenge.

I had been there a few times, and she always made me some of this coffee, and on one visit, when she asked if I would like a cup, I replied, 'Yes, please. It's all I come here for, you know; shoeing your pony is only secondary to this super coffee.' She was quite pleased with that comment, and I repeated it at intervals of a few visits for quite some time.

The time came when I met the husband for the first time. He came out to see to the pony, and he didn't like the idea of having to stand with it; he didn't like the idea of shoeing it where I had always shod it; he didn't like the idea of me doing the shoeing; in fact, he didn't seem to like the idea of anything at all. When his wife brought the coffee out, he didn't like that either, and his face showed his displeasure, even though he didn't say anything about it. I met him on very rare occasions during the years of shoeing for the family, and the fewer the better as far as I was concerned, because I couldn't stand the sight of the man.

On one occasion when I arrived to shoe the pony, he came out to see to it and said to me, 'There won't be any of that lovely coffee for you today, my wife has been ill in bed for a fortnight.'

I said how sorry I was to hear that his wife was ill, and said I hoped she would soon be up and about again. I didn't realise how soon that was going to be. I had got about halfway through the job of shoeing the pony, when out came the lady of the house with the coffee – and she hadn't been out of bed for a fortnight.

Well! As you can imagine, the husband's face went black as a thundercloud. He looked as if he might have a stroke at any moment. I didn't know where to look or what to say, I was so embarrassed. I have no idea what was said after I left, but that was the last time I ever went to that pony. Surprise, surprise…

Pus-I'-Foot

I received a rather frantic telephone call from a customer one day, asking me to go and look at her horse which, she said, was very lame. This was not long after the advent of the Farrier's Registration Council, and I had just received the 'Farrier's Code of Practice', which stated that farriers must not diagnose or treat lamenesses.

I explained this to my customer, and advised her to get the vet over to see to it. She said the vet had just left, and told her to see if her farrier would attend; she also said that, when she had telephoned her vets, they had sent out a young chap who seemed to be frightened to death of touching the horse. She was worried sick about it, because the horse was down, waving its leg about in the air, obviously in great distress.

I thought, *To hell with the FRC and the Code of Practice, this horse needs help.* It wasn't as if I had never done these jobs before; I'd been doing them for donkey's years. So, as soon as I had finished the shoeing that I was doing, I set off to see to this lame horse.

Even after all the years of dealing with lameness, whenever I went to a lame horse, I would hope that it would turn out to be one of the easy ones, as sometimes it is extremely difficult to find exactly where the problem is. Well, just like the lady customer had said, the horse was down and obviously in great pain, and it was not difficult to tell which leg was hurting it; it was just a question of finding the source of the lameness. I said to the horse, 'Come on, old lad, let's see what we can do about it for thi.'

So I started at the knee, squeezing gently, and worked my way down the leg feeling for heat, or any sign of trouble, but there was nothing until I got to the foot. The foot was quite warm to the touch, which was no surprise, as 95% of lameness in horses is in the foot, and now all that remained to be done was to find the exact spot; easier said than done, as the horse flinched at every part of the foot. So, I scraped round with my paring knife to see if I could find any telltale black marks that could lead to an abscess. There were a few likely looking places, but one in particular caught my eye — right at the tip of the toe, and just inside the white line — so I started to dig. It was soon evident that this was the right place, as the more I dug, the further the black mark tracked upwards.

The lady owner was getting even more worried as time went on, and kept asking if I had found anything yet. I told her that I thought that I had found the problem, but that it was going to be a difficult job finding the entry place, as it seemed to be right up the hoof wall.

'Oh, is it going to be all right?' she asked, quite frantically.

'I certainly hope so,' I replied, feeling anything but full of confidence.

I had started to cut through the wall of the hoof by now, as I couldn't get any further from underneath, and this was a very time-consuming operation, and the lady was getting more anxious by the minute.

'Have you found it yet? Oh, I think you ought to stop… is it going to be all right?' were some of the things she said.

'I am tracking the abscess up inside the wall, and I must keep going until I get either pus or blood,' I told her, 'and preferably pus.'

By this time, I had got about two inches up the wall, and still the black mark was tracking upwards, and even I was beginning to have doubts. After another couple of cuts, there was a slight 'pop' and a stream of black pus shot out right across the stable.

'Oh! What was that?' cried the owner, almost hysterically.

'That's the jackpot,' I said, 'a load of beautiful pus!'

'What's beautiful about pus?' my customer asked.

'It's beautiful because your troubles are over for this time, and your horse will be on its feet in a few minutes,' I assured her.

'Are you sure — you're not having me on, are you?' she asked.

'Would I do that to you?' I asked.

'Yes, you would,' she said, 'I've known you a long time.'

In reply to that, the horse struggled to its feet, and I said, 'Now who's having you on?'

The lady was delighted and relieved that it was all over, and couldn't thank me enough. I must say that I also was quite relieved, and very pleased to get that good result, after all the hard work I had put in.

The Runaways

Someone rang one day wanting some trims doing. The trouble with trims is, you don't know what you are supposed to trim, whether it's brood stock, donkeys, Shetland ponies, shires or old, retired riders. Anyway, I went.

When I arrived, I was met by a rather large, corpulent fellow, who said that the horses to be trimmed were out in a field. If there is one thing that sounds the alarm bells, it's 'The horses are out in the field, we'll do them there.' Moreover, he didn't look like a horse person. I don't mean by this that he wasn't wearing Barbour and ratting cap; he just looked as if he would be more at home sitting and watching television.

So we went to the field, and he duly caught one of the animals to be trimmed. It was a thoroughbred mare, about sixteen hands, which looked to be quite pregnant. He brought it over to the gate where I was waiting, and climbed up and sat on the top bar of the wooden gate. I picked a hind leg up to make a start, and the mare started hopping sideways and pulling against me, which is nothing new, and I just hung on and started to work on the feet. The horse pulled and pushed, pulled and pushed, but I hung on and kept clipping and cutting, until I noticed that the horse's head was not in the place that it was supposed to be, that is, in the middle of the gate where the chap was supposed to be sitting. Its head had moved to the left, allowing the horse to drag me about, so I turned to see what had happened, and I saw the fat man running away across the next field — he had left me holding onto a hind foot with the horse at liberty to do just as it pleased!

I never found out the reason why he legged it, I just assumed that he hadn't any experience of working closely with horses, and thought it was just a case of 'all horses are born having their feet dressed, and they always stand perfectly still throughout the procedure'. Farriery would be a very much easier job if that were the case.

I had another very similar case at another location, where the owner was a young woman who had acquired a brown and white cob, but this time she wanted it shoeing.

My first impression of the woman was that she didn't seem like a horse person; in fact, I wondered if she knew which end was front, as she seemed to have no idea how to handle the horse. She had managed to bring the horse (another mare) to the meeting place, which was a short, narrow, cobbled cul-de-sac, with a mill on one side, cottages on the other side and a wall at the far end – and nowhere to tie the horse. I asked her to stand in what I thought would be the best place, from my point of view, and to stick hold of it and stand her ground, no matter what. I started as I always do, on a hind foot, and, just like the previous horse, it pulled, then pushed, pulled then pushed. But this was nothing out of the ordinary as far as I was concerned, and I just stuck hold and kept working.

Quite suddenly, the horse seemed to be moving about a lot more than it should have been able to do, and I looked round to see why. I caught sight of the young woman just disappearing into one of the cottages, leaving me to stop the mare running off, by holding onto a hind leg – not the best way of controlling a horse, you might say. I had to let go of the leg, and nip round quickly to stop the horse from running out of the cul-de-sac onto the road. I then had to keep hold of the mare while I went and knocked on the door for the frightened young woman to come and see to her horse. She came out reluctantly, drying her tears, and said, 'I'm sorry, I didn't expect it to be like that.'

I thought, *Like what? Nothing's happened yet... what would you do if the going got rough*? Instead, I tried to reassure her that the horse's behaviour was quite common, and there was nothing to be afraid of. Anyway, I managed to get the job done and muttered quietly, 'Here endeth the first lesson.'

The Bakers

I used to do a lot of work in one particular area, and soon got to know where all the best sandwich shops were, and I would even go a bit out of my way at lunch time to buy a sandwich from one of my favourite shops. There was one place that was the best of all. It belonged to a rather portly (read 'fat') chap, who shambled rather than walked, but who baked his own bread and teacakes and cooked the joints of meat. But best of all, he cut the meat with the knife — not one of those machines that slice it so thin that you're not quite sure what sort of sandwich you ordered. When you asked for a ham sandwich, you got a nice thick slice of ham, which always tasted like ham used to do before the advent of injecting water, double wrapping and the obsession with hygiene.

Also, at the time of this tale, there were no such things as double yellow lines in the road, and if you wanted to go to a shop, you parked outside it if you were on that side of the road, or directly opposite if you were going the other way.

I had been in this shop several times before and got to know the owner quite well — well enough to pass the time of day and comment on the weather, anyway. On this particular day, I parked across the road from the shop, and as I jumped out of my vehicle, I saw the shopkeeper look across, and as my vehicle had my name and occupation in rather large letters on each side, he obviously knew who I was, and what I did for a living. I went inside and there were a couple of women waiting to be served, and in that place this meant more than a short wait, as the owner was very steady. As soon as I was through the door, he said in rather a loud voice, 'There's a strong smell of horse shit in here!' So I answered, 'Well, wash your hands then, and make me a ham sandwich.' I got a glower from him and a smile from the waiting women; I also got my nice thick sandwich.

Which reminds me of the time I went into a baker's shop in another town. It was a particularly cold day, and I was wearing a rather thick woolly jumper. I had just finished shoeing a horse, and the smell from the burning horn lingered quite heavily in the thick jumper.

As I entered the shop, there were a few women waiting to be served, and I could see their noses start twitching, and I smiled quietly to myself. After a few minutes, when the smell had registered with the lady behind the counter, she called out to someone in the back room, 'Is there a knife handle burning on the stove?'

'No,' was the reply, 'I don't know what that smell can be.'

I got my sandwich and beat a hasty retreat, taking the smell with me, but probably leaving a lingering odour behind. Life has its simple pleasures.

Prince's Wedges

The first time I shod Prince for her lady owner, she said a bit fussily, 'You must put heel wedges on.'

'Oh, why's that, then?' I asked.

'Well, if he gets to the bottom of the field [which was quite steep] I can't get him back up, because his stifle slips out if he doesn't have wedges on,' she said.

'Right, I'll have a look and see if anything can be done about it,' I answered.

'Well, don't forget, he must have them on,' she insisted.

The cure for the stifle, or kneecap slipping out, is to raise the heels; but, if the heels had not been cut off in the first place, there would be no need to raise them. So I had a good look, and sure enough, the heels were far too low, so I put plastic heel wedges under the hind shoes as an emergency measure, until the natural heels had recovered sufficiently, and told the owner that if I let the heels grow without cutting them for a couple of shoeings, I should then be able to leave the wedges off and there should be no more stifle trouble.

'Oh, you can't leave them off,' she said, 'or I'll never get him up the field again.'

The next time I shod him, she reminded me in no uncertain terms that Prince *must* have wedges on. I saw no reason to argue with her, as the heels had not recovered sufficiently in that time, so wedges were duly fitted and the dear lady was pacified.

After two more visits, I thought the time had arrived when I could try it without the wedges, so I told my customer that I was going to leave them off, as the heels were by now more than half an inch higher than when I first saw them. Well, she nearly had a heart attack and said, 'No, no, you can't leave them off, we'll never get him up the field.'

I explained that the heels were by now half an inch higher than before, and the wedges are only about three-eighths of an inch thick, so the heels were higher now without the wedges than they had been *with* them previously. It made no difference; she was adamant, so wedges again it was.

However, the next time I shod the horse, I just left them off and said nothing, but braced myself for the backlash. She didn't notice, and I left them off a second time and she still didn't notice. A couple of weeks after leaving the wedges off for the second time, I was at the same yard shoeing someone else's horse when the lady came up to me and said, 'How long has my Prince been without wedges?'

'Oh, about three months now. Why, are you having problems again?' I asked.

'That's just it,' she said. 'He's been perfectly all right, and I think you are sneaky for leaving the wedges off without telling me!'

'If I had told you, you would never have slept again, would you?' I asked.

'No, I suppose you're right, but I still think you are sneaky,' she replied with a touch of pretend hurt in her voice.

'I had no other way of assessing the situation, and I needed to know whether my treatment had worked or not,' I told her.

'Well, it did,' she said, and walked off quite pleased about it all.

Another satisfied customer.

Keeping Up with the Joneses

I used to shoe a little jumping horse for a young lad who was still a schoolboy at the time. He was a nice lad, who seemed to me to be a bit shy, but he must have been a very good rider, because he seemed to do a lot of winning. I must have shod the horse for him ten or a dozen times, and he was always telling me that he had won this and that class, so it was obviously performing satisfactorily.

The horse in question belonged to someone else, I found out later, and one day when I arrived to shoe it, the lad said that the owner wanted me to put plastic heel wedges on the front feet. Now, I had nothing against these heel wedges, as long as I felt that they were justified, and there was no other way of curing whatever problem needed raised heels. However, this horse was obviously performing all right, if it was doing all the winning the lad said it was; so I pointed this out to him and said that I didn't want to use wedges, as it didn't need them.

'It's the owner,' he said, 'and he wants them on.'

'Well, tell the owner that I say it's not a good idea, as it seems to be performing OK without them.' Anyway, I shod it without.

The next time I went to shoe this horse the owner himself was there, and he said that he wanted these wedges on. I asked him what made him want wedges on when the animal was obviously jumping all right as it was.

'Well, So-and-so's horses all have them on,' he said, naming a famous showjumper of the time, 'and if they're good enough for him, they're good enough for me.'

'Ah, so that's what this is all about,' I said. 'It's all about keeping up with the Joneses and not about necessity.'

'Well, I want them on,' he said, 'all So-and-so's have them on.'

I told him that that may be the case, but as I didn't shoe for So-and-so, he was at liberty to do whatever he pleased with his horses' feet, and it was none of my business; but in this case, heel wedges were totally unnecessary, and would be detrimental to the welfare of the horse, and I did not want to put them on.

'Well, I want them on,' came the reply.

'OK,' I said, 'but the responsibility is your own.'

So I did as he requested and shod the horse with wedges.

The next time I went to shoe it, there were no wedges to take off, so I asked the young chap where they were.

'I jumped at a show the day after you put them on,' he said. 'I jumped the first line of fences, and I couldn't get the horse to turn at the corner of the course, and it ran straight on into the fence, and it was like that for the whole round, and I ended up eliminated. So I took it to the course farrier and asked him to take the wedges off, and I went on to win the next two classes.'

'What does the owner say to that then?' I asked.

'I haven't seen hide or hair of him,' the young chap said.

Yes, I thought, *that's about right*.

Midnight Farrier

I once received a telephone call at about ten o'clock at night, from a very good customer, asking me to go over to his place to have a look at a lame horse. I said that I would come first thing in the morning, which meant eight o'clock.

'No, no,' he said, 'I want you to come over now.'

'But it's ten o'clock already, and it'll take me an hour to get there, and anyway, you should be calling the vet, not me,' I told him.

'The vet has just this minute gone,' he said, 'and he hasn't been able to find anything wrong with it, but the horse is hopping lame, and I'm worried sick about it. It's my best horse, and I paid five thousand pounds for it. I don't want anything to happen to it, and I'd like you to come now.'

This was twenty-five years ago, and five grand was a lot of money for a horse then. So I said, 'OK, I'll set off now, but it will be about eleven o'clock when I get there.' As I have already stated, he was a very good customer, but I thought, *The bloody horse had better be hopping lame, dragging me out at this time of night!*

So I put my steel toe-capped boots on again — I never went out to horses without toe protection — found the best torch I had, and off I went. All other necessary tackle was always in the truck. The reason for the good torch was that I have yet to go to a stable after dark where you could see the horse easily, never mind do close work on it.

When I arrived at the stable, sure enough, the horse was hopping lame, in fact it was waving the offending foot about, and was obviously in distress. Judging by its behaviour, the trouble was an abscess. There was no point in looking for anything else, so I pressed carefully round the sole of the foot with my thumb in an attempt to locate the source of the trouble, and to my surprise I found it easily enough. It was then just a question of scraping gently to remove dirt and surface tissue, and sure enough, there was the telltale tiny black mark which meant that the sole had been pierced. I dug gently with my paring knife, and suddenly out popped about a thimbleful of evil-smelling black pus.

I felt the horse heave a sigh of relief, and by the time I had finished squeezing the wound to make sure all the pus was out, and let go of the leg, the horse stood on the lame leg straight away.

'You will need to poultice the foot for a couple of days, just to make sure that all the rubbish is out,' I said to the owner.

'How do I do that?' he asked, so I had to get stuck in and show him what every horse owner should know — that is, how to make a bran poultice.

Anyway, he was delighted that his horse was going to be all right, but it was midnight by this time, and I had to be up by six thirty to start my next day's (or same day's) work. It was going to be a long and hard one!

The Dealer

'Can ta cum and shiew us sum 'ossis?' said the voice on the telephone.

'Where are you and how many?' I asked.

He told me where, and said there would be 'aboot twenty er so'. I thought, *We've got a right joker here*, so I said, 'OK, I'll pop up now and do them before bedtime.' It was about nine o'clock at night.

'Oh, I'm not joking,' said the voice. 'There'll be at least twenty, mebby twenty-two.'

I hadn't been working on my own account for very long, and found it difficult to believe that one person could want twenty horses shoeing all at one go. Anyway, I arranged to go and do them, wondering what I was letting myself in for. As things turned out, I had let myself in for a very good customer indeed. I did twenty-two over two days on that visit, and he explained that the farrier he'd been using had lost his driving licence to the demon drink, and he needed someone to replace him. I said, 'Look no further, you've just found him.'

He was a dealer, and would buy horses by the fieldful over the telephone without seeing them, send a few wagons for them, swing them, break them in to a reasonable degree, then sell them on, giving the buyer my telephone number along with the horse. Thanks to this system I picked up a good clientele in that area, which lasted for many years. I would go to the dealer's yard every other Wednesday and shoe whatever he had to do, usually about ten, and this went on for quite a few years. When I had finished the shoeing he would say, 'Haa mich does ta want?' and would

85

dive a hand into his overalls pocket and pull out a handful of crumpled notes, with the odd fiver dropping on the ground, and pay me up there and then. His favourite saying was, 'When tha gits sum shiews on 'em, it liewks as if they've dun summat.'

He bought all sorts of ruffians, and sometimes proceedings became a bit rough, but they had to have 'shiews' on, no matter what.

Over the years, I picked up a lot of customers in that area, and I would arrange to do all of them on the same day — but not Wednesdays as they were kept for my dealer-man — and after a while it got to be as much a social visit as a working one. I would leave home at seven o'clock in the morning, and get back late in the evening on those days. They were long days, but usually quite enjoyable, with cups of tea and a good natter at each place, which made all the hard work seem worthwhile. Although many years have passed, I still see one or two of my old customers at shows up and down, and we always have a good chat.

The Double-barrelled Cannon

I was called to the yard of a haulage contractor to shoe a Shetland pony many years ago. I have mentioned in previous stories how much I hate shoeing Shetlands, and this story is one of the main reasons why.

When I arrived at the yard, the pony was tied up to the sturdy handle of a large, heavy steel garage door, which I considered adequate. However, there was nobody about, and nobody came out to see who had just driven into the yard. Anyway, I thought I would make a start, and someone was sure to appear soon.

I approached the Shetland to have a look at its feet from the front, and it took no notice of me, so I assumed it was used to people, and I hoped it was used to being shod. I got my shoeing box out of the van, and started to put my apron on. As soon as the apron appeared, the pony started showing signs of restlessness, and began moving from side to side, snorting and pawing the ground, and I thought, *This could be a bit nasty, you'd better watch yourself.* I approached the pony again to start dressing its feet, and it deliberately lined its back end in my direction and bucked a bit, so I moved to the side, and the back end followed; I moved to the other side and the back end followed… it was like lining up a cannon, ready to give me a double barrel! I feinted to one side, and as the pony moved in that direction, I nipped smartly up the other side, so that I was standing to the side of the pony in relative safety, and I reached for a foot. Strangely enough, it didn't make much to-do about actually having its feet dressed, and I managed to get all four ready to receive shoes; but to get the shoes ready meant going back to my van and leaving the side of the pony and safety.

I got the first shoe hot and shaped, and went for the first try, but the cannon was lined up exactly, and I could see that it was ready to fire, so I thought that I would try to fool it again by making for one side, then nipping back up the other side before it could realign. But the crafty pony was ready for that, and wasn't going to be fooled again, and as I changed direction, the pony lashed out with a blood-curdling scream. Both hind feet hit me in the most tender part of my body, and I dropped like a sack of spuds. And still nobody had appeared.

I lay there for a while until I came round a bit, and then I walked stiffly back to my van and put my tools away, and thought, *Well, you shouldn't have even started that job when you saw how it behaved as soon as it saw the apron. You got what you asked for!* That didn't make me feel any better, but at least it was honest.

My reproductive organs ached for a month after that, and that is the real reason why I always hated Shetland ponies; and whenever I was asked to work on one, I always thought, *Please let it be a good one...* but they rarely were.

A Close Call

There is a breed of horses which are yellow and white in colour, and they are usually cob types, and always 'good doers', that is to say that they easily get very fat, with a huge crest on the neck, and round, barrel-shaped bodies.

Strangely enough, in my experience, the owners never seem to recognise that their horses are overweight, and it is quite common for this breed to be prone to laminitis, especially in spring and summer when there is an abundance of grass. The trouble is, they are turned out in a field for six days a week, and ridden for an hour on the seventh day – if it doesn't rain – and they spend the rest of their lives eating. This type of horse seems to be attractive to owners who don't want to ride much, and they always seem to end up with the same problem – laminitis, inflammation of the tissue inside the hoof – sooner or later.

From the point of view of shoeing them, they are no different to any other breed; but as soon as they start putting weight on, they become quite difficult to handle. In fact sometimes they become downright nasty.

When you tell the owner that the horse is too fat, and it's that that's making them difficult, they invariably say (indignantly), 'My horse isn't too fat, I think it looks lovely!' Although it has a great thick neck, and a deep cleft at the base of the spine above the root of the tail, which are sure indications of obesity.

I went to shoe one of these 'yeller-'uns' (as I refer to them) on one particular day, and yes, it was obese, as it had been turned out all winter and done nothing but eat for several months, and it had been brought out of the field especially to be shod. I arrived early in the morning, and the farmer who owned the horse was busy milking. The children, who had caught the horse, were getting ready for school, leaving it tied to a gate in a stony lane for me to manage as best I could, seemingly. (Ah, facilities!)

Anyway, I made a start, but the horse made it quite clear right from the off that it didn't want to be there, and it pulled, pushed and hopped round, with me hanging onto a leg, trying to dress a foot, and with the stones underfoot it was difficult for me to keep my balance. The horse hopped round until I was squashed against the wall, which made dressing its feet even more difficult. I managed to get them done eventually, and got the new shoes fitted, which was quite a difficult task, as the feet became chipped by the stones underfoot, and seemed to be a different shape each time I picked them up. I was eventually ready to start nailing on, but when I picked a hind foot up, the horse pushed me up against the wall and leaned on me so hard that it was just about impossible to work. I would get a couple of nails in a shoe with great difficulty, then let go, push my way out, and try the other side. The horse would hop round and squash me against the wall at the other side; but I would manage to get some nails in before I had to let go, and eventually I got them all in.

Unfortunately, all this squashing me against the wall had loosened some stones, and as the horse pressed me against the wall for the umpteenth time, I felt the wall give way — but it was slipping *towards* me, and I couldn't get out of the way. I didn't want either myself or the horse injured, so I let go of the leg very slowly, but kept pushing against the wall in an attempt to hold it up while I shouted for the farmer to come and take the horse out of the way. Eventually, he heard me shouting, and came to see what was wrong. I asked him to take the horse out of the way.

'Why?' he asked.

'Take the horse out of the way and you will soon see,' I replied.

As soon as the horse was clear, I jumped away from the wall, and about four feet of it crashed into the lane. 'Now you know why,' I said.

Fortunately, nobody was hurt, but it had been a close call.

Puddled

This story concerns a family, one of whom rang to ask if I would shoe three showjumping ponies. I said yes, I would, and was given directions to their yard.

When I arrived to do the job, I saw that the place was undergoing renovation from what looked to have been a derelict farm. The house part had had a lot of work done on it, and I could see that it would soon be a splendid property. The yard had also had some work done, as it looked to have been cleared and levelled, but the first thing that caught my eye was that there didn't seem to be a decent surface to stand the ponies on whilst they were being shod. The yard had been covered with two-inch limestone chippings, which is about the last kind of surface you want to shoe horses on. I asked the daughter, who seemed to be in charge, if there was anywhere else to work, explaining that the ponies would not be able to stand on this size of very sharp chippings, and when they had the old shoes removed, the feet would be cut and chipped and it would be difficult to do a decent job. So she suggested the laithe porch, which was flagged (with big gaps in between the flags) but was just large enough to stand a pony cornerways. I said it would be a bit tight, but I would try and manage. So, I made a start on the first pony, taking the old shoes off and dressing the feet, ready for the new shoes.

The trouble began when I stood on a certain flag, and a jet of mucky cold water shot straight up my trouser leg. Well, you can put up with all sorts of difficulties when there is only one horse to shoe, but I had three to do, and I would have to stand on this flag umpteen times to complete the job, and as I had no choice of anywhere else to stand, I looked like getting a soaking.

I tried standing a bit askew, which was all right if the pony stood still, but how many ponies stand still whilst being shod? Every time I had to move to keep my balance, I would tread on this flag, and the water would shoot up my leg. I eventually completed the job, and by that time my leg was wet, my trouser leg was dripping water, my sock was soaked and my boot was almost full of this awful water, and I was a bit miffed (quite an understatement). The daughter asked if I would go again, and I said I would, but I would like a better place to work.

I didn't hear from them again, but quite a while later, one of my other customers asked what I had been saying to the girl. Her father had asked who shod for them, and when my other customer told him it was me, he had said, 'Oh, we're not having him again, he told my daughter our place was not fit to work in' − which was not quite the same thing as what I had either said or meant, but at least I didn't have to go there and get puddled again.

It Takes Two

When I started shoeing for a particular family of farmers, the children were only small and there were a couple of 12.2 ponies to do. As the kids grew and became more proficient, the parents bought bigger and better ponies, to enable the kids to compete in Pony Club activities.

I had been going to them for a few years, when I was asked to trim the feet of the brood stock. This was a complete surprise to me, as I didn't know they had any brood stock. Anyway I said yes, I would do them, and the mother said she would let me know when they could get them in. I thought that a bit strange, but the family had been good customers for a long time, so it was left like that. The call came, and I arranged to go and do the job. Well, I had never seen such an unruly looking bunch as I encountered that day. They were quite wild, as they spent all their lives running out on the moors, and were only brought in for special purposes. The farmer had them penned in the yard and they were milling round. They quite obviously didn't like the idea of being where they were, and I had to trim their feet.

The only decent place to stand them was on a raised causeway about four feet wide, with a 3-foot-high garden wall at one side and a foot deep drop at the other, and a mistal door handle to tie them to: facilities to dream about. I managed to get one or two done, with the lady standing at the other side of the garden wall, until we got the pony that wasn't going to be done — there's always one. It kicked and reared and carried on, but I managed to get the hind feet done. When I reached for a front foot, it reared with a

94

mighty heave and broke the tying-up rope, so I tried to duck away under its flailing front feet, and as I straightened up the pony came down with one foot on each of my shoulders; it must have looked as if we were doing the tango! Anyway, I heaved it off and pushed it over backwards, and said to the lady, 'This is getting a bit ridiculous!' To which she replied — still at the other side of the wall — 'You must get them worse than this.'

I have never found out just how difficult things have to be before an owner admits to having animals that are not fit to be handled.

It always seems to me that people think farriers are a bit like Jesus in the parable of the fishermen when the storm was raging, and he said, 'Peace, be still,' and the storm abated. We are supposed to place hands on the unruly horses and say, 'Peace, be still,' and they are suddenly transformed into calm, amenable animals! Sadly, it doesn't work like that.

The next day was Sunday and I was playing in my brass band at Peasholme Park in Scarborough. When I put my euphonium mouthpiece to my lips, I found that they were bruised — that pony must have smacked me in the mouth during its antics. So instead of having a pleasant afternoon's music making, I had a painful afternoon trying to make music — which is not quite the same thing. But needless to say, there must be worse things happen in the course of doing one's job.

In Yorkshire Now

This story concerns a lady who had moved into this area, and needed her horse shoeing, and wondered if I would do it for her. I said that I would, and made an arrangement to go and see to it for her. When I arrived, the horse was tied up in the barn, munching away contentedly on a hay net.

First impressions of a new owner are very important in the horse shoeing business, and I was quite pleased to see the horse standing perfectly at ease, and the owner moving round it with what seemed to be a very easy rapport. However, there was one thing that immediately took my eye, and that was the bucket of food that was evident against the wall. After many years' experience of the effect that food has on animal behaviour, the alarm bells sounded, and I asked the lady why there was a bucket of food where the horse could see it. She said, 'Ah – it doesn't like the hind shoes nailing on, and it needs the food to take its mind off it.'

I thought, *Oh shit*, having been in this position many times before. I knew that this was Trouble, as you have noticed, with a capital 'T'. So I said to the lady, 'I would like the food round the corner out of sight.'

She said, 'But it won't have the hind shoes nailed on without eating.'

'We'll cross that bridge when we get there,' I said.

We chatted some more and I asked the lady where she had come from. She said, 'Stoke on Trent,' and I said, 'Ah, pot wallahs and all that.'

She seemed quite amused by that, and I thought, *We've got a nice lass here*. Anyway, we chatted as I got on with the main job of shoeing the horse, and we seemed to get on quite well; but I knew when the trouble would start, and it wasn't so much a question of 'when' as 'how much'. I was very experienced in this sort of thing, so I was not really bothered, the only question was the reaction of the owner when the storm broke.

I have always followed a system when doing my job, and that is: remove all shoes and dress all feet, fit all shoes, whether new or replaced, nail on, then clench up and finish. If you have a system, you never have to think where you have got to. In this case, I dressed all of the feet, fitted three new shoes, and had almost finished fitting the fourth shoe, when I said to the lady, 'Do you mind making me a cup of tea, I haven't had a drink all day, and I'm nearly gagged.' It was the middle of the afternoon, and I had had several cuppas, but she didn't know that.

'Of course I will,' she replied, 'but are you sure you will be all right?'

'I'll be OK,' I said. 'If there's a problem I'll wait until you come back,' I added, lying through my back teeth.

By the time she had got into the house, I was ready to start nailing on, and I asked the horse for a hind foot, but as soon as hammer hit nail, the horse lashed out. I was ready for this, and I dropped the foot and gave it a taste of its own medicine. I started again, and the same thing happened again: as soon as hammer hit nail − *bang*. So I gave it another taste of its own medicine − 'Aunty Maggie's Remedy', which I referred to earlier − and it almost always takes two doses. Anyway, it must have liked the flavour, because it suddenly forgot its bad manners, and stood as gentle as a lamb from then on.

When the lady appeared with the cuppa, I had both hind shoes nailed on, and was on with the first front one. 'How did you manage to get the hind shoes on without the bucket of food?' she asked incredulously.

'You are in Yorkshire now,' I said, 'not Stoke on Trent, and the air is different up here.'

Anyway, the horse seemed to like the air, for there was never any more bother with nailing on hind shoes again.

April

No, not the month, but the horse.

April was one of those funny-coloured, roan, Appaloosa-type horses, and a mare to boot — which didn't make things any easier. She was absolutely stone quiet to work on; you could groom her, ride her, lead her, catch her or dress her feet without a bit of bother, but as soon as hammer touched nail, she decided that that was more than she was having, and she became quite difficult. She would kick out, pull back, push, shove, squash me against the wall, and a few more tricks that I can't remember; but the only thing that was certain was, she was not going to have shoes nailed on her feet. The trouble with this horse was that I shod about thirty horses in that yard, and if you do the quiet ones, you do the others as well — no matter how difficult, so it had to be done.

Well, this was difficult, but with perseverance, a lot of muscle, and a bit of luck, I used to manage to get it shod, but I used to dread seeing its name on the shoeing list. I had the pleasure of doing it for a couple of years, but one day when I arrived to do my weekly stint, the yard owner said, 'You'll be pleased to know that April has gone. The owners have sold it.' I wasn't so much pleased as absolutely delighted.

A few weeks later, I was driving through a neighbouring town, when I happened to spot what looked like April in a field at the side of the road. I thought, *Ah! I know where you are now, and if there is a call from someone new in this area, I will know to avoid it at all costs.* Well, I didn't get any calls, but I noticed a couple of months later that the horse was no longer in that field, and its memory faded away.

A long time later, probably more than a year, I received a telephone call from a new customer many miles from the two places where I had encountered April, asking if I would go and shoe a horse at their place, so I agreed to go. When I arrived, I saw that there were quite a few horses on the property, and I wondered why they wanted me (I always had a suspicious mind) as obviously someone else was shoeing there. The horse I had to shoe was a funny-coloured, roan, Appaloosa-type mare, which was standing tied up in a nice clean place, munching quite peacefully on a hay net.

I had forgotten all about April after all this time, and I set about shoeing this mare, which stood like a sheep through the foot dressing, shoe fitting, including smoke from the burning hoof, and of course I was lulled into believing that all was well with the world. *But*, as soon as I hit the first nail with the hammer, it was like a different animal, and it went crackers. *Then* I remembered April, and *then* I knew why I was there, because the other chap wouldn't do it — or more likely couldn't do it.

However, I got it done (I had put too much work in to leave without pay) and charged the new owner double my normal fee, and asked where the horse had come from. Sure enough, it was April, so I asked the owner why she had called me when she already had a farrier.

'Well, he couldn't shoe it,' she said, 'so I asked the previous owner who had shod it, and they gave me your name.'

Well, I was a bit miffed at being used as a punchbag, so I said to the lady, 'I don't like being used like this. You owners don't care who gets hurt so long as you get shoes on your horse, and don't ever call me again under any circumstances.'

I don't like that sort of animal in a big yard where there is little choice but to shoe them, but I'll be damned if I'll do them where somebody else is doing all the easy ones!

Welsh Cobs

I used to go to a place where they bred Section D Welsh cobs. Beautiful animals; the brood mares were black with white blaze and white legs, really good-looking stock. Some of the progeny were black, some dark bay, some were chestnut, but they were all fine examples of Section D Welsh.

The first time I went to dress their feet, the owner had them all in what was a fairly large yard, surrounded by loose boxes, and there was a tying-up ring in a right-angled corner. That arrangement was good because there was a wall to get them up against at each side, which meant they didn't have so much room to jump about in. Also, keeping them all together meant that they still had each other's company, which in turn meant better behaviour. These simple measures made life just a bit easier, as you had a bit more control of the unruly brood stock, which didn't get much in the way of handling. This first time I managed to get all the feet dressed without too much bother; you never get away entirely scot-free with brood stock, but I couldn't really complain this time.

The next time I went, there was no sign of horses in the yard, and when I asked where they were, the owner said, 'Oh, we'll do them in the field.'

'I don't think so,' I answered. 'We will have a much better chance up here in the yard like last time, as there is somewhere to tie them up, and a corner to restrict their movement.'

'What's the matter with you?' was the reply to that. 'I've got a chap coming who can hold them.'

I said, 'The chap hasn't been born yet who can hold a Section D cob if it doesn't want to be held.'

Again, he asked what was the matter with me, and so I said, 'Right, say no more, we'll do them in the field; but don't forget, you have been warned.'

'You must be getting soft,' was the rather scathing reply; but I held my tongue, and we set off in his Land Rover to the field where this 'chap who could hold them' was waiting. He was about six feet tall and well-built, and wore a flat cap and glasses. He looked to be a handy enough chap, but not handy enough for the job in hand.

Anyway, they caught up a three-year-old chestnut which hadn't been handled at all. It was a lovely looking horse, with white blaze and white socks.

'How do you like this one, then?' asked the owner.

'It's a good-looking horse,' I answered, as I approached the youngster. 'But I'll tell you how I like it when I've got its feet dressed.'

As I got close to it, it started to circle the 'chap who could hold them', and the more I followed, the faster it circled. So I made a grab for a front foot, in the hope that it would stop for a while. As soon as I touched its leg it just reared up and smacked the 'chap who could hold them' in the middle of the forehead, and laid him out cold, with his cap and glasses askew.

'Now where's your big man who's going to hold them?' I asked.

'Ee, well, I didn't expect it to do that!' spluttered the owner.

'No, and you wouldn't listen either, would you,' I reminded him. 'I've been in this situation many times before, but you owners seem to think I must have lived in a monastery or something, and know nothing about this job.'

'Happen we'd best leave them, and get them up in the yard for another time,' he suggested, somewhat chastened. I have always said that the best lessons are learnt the hard way.

Welsh Section A

Shortly after the Welsh cobs episode, this same owner acquired a Section A Welsh pony and rang for me to go and shoe it ready for showing at the weekend. When I arrived the owner said that he wanted the biggest, heaviest shoes that I could manage to get on. I couldn't believe this, and told him that he needed the lightest shoes – like aluminium – for showing a Section A; or better still, just have the feet trimmed and no shoes at all, to allow the pony to show its natural grace of movement in the show ring.

'No,' he said, 'I want the biggest shoes you can get on it, they'll make it throw its feet out.'

I said, 'Look, I can put shoes on that it won't be able to lift' – exaggerating somewhat – 'but you will be just wasting my time and your money having it done like that, and you may as well stay at home as go to a show with that sort of shoe on.'

As with the Section Ds in the last story, he complained that I thought I knew best all the time, and so I said, 'Well, I do this for a living, not for fun, and if I don't know, who does?'

So off he went in the house and telephoned an experienced show pony owner, complaining that I wouldn't put heavy shoes on his Section A pony. When he came out of the house, he looked a bit grim and said, 'Put aluminium shoes on it, then!' No apology or acknowledgement that I had been right. Anyway, the pony went on to win a few classes, and then straight away he became an overnight expert on show pony shoeing. Ah, Education is a wonderful thing!

Reasoning

This is the story of a pony that I shod for many years as the daughters of the house grew up. There were two ponies involved, but one was quite a bit older than the other, and as things turned out, a bit more wily.

The house where they lived was a beautiful place, with a large, very well-kept garden. There were lawns that were always well mown with beautifully trimmed edges; there were rose beds, herbaceous borders, shrubs, a vegetable plot and an orchard. The stable block, with about six boxes and tack room, divided the gardens from the field where the ponies were kept.

When the daughters were at school, the ponies were well ridden, probably most nights after school, and Pony Club activities at the weekends, so they were usually quite well behaved when it came to shoeing time.

However, when the girls went to university, things changed considerably. The ponies were not being ridden much and spent all their lives eating grass and generally doing exactly as they pleased. One time when I went to dress their feet, the girls' mother caught them and put them in one of the boxes for me to see to, and left me to get on. I caught the younger one, put a head collar on, and tied it to the usual ring in the wall where I had tied them each time I had shod them in the past. It didn't seem to like having its liberty curtailed, and proceeded to pull back against the rope in the hope of regaining its freedom. It wasn't very persistent however, and when it found out that liberty was not going to be easily gained, it gave up pulling and allowed me to get on and trim its feet.

I put that one back in the box, and caught the other one — the older, more wily one. I took it outside and tied it to the same ring in the wall. It too, decided that it didn't want to be there, and proceeded to pull at the rope; only this one was more determined to get away, and it really laid back and pulled, shaking its head as it did so, and finally the rope could hold no longer, and parted suddenly, sitting the pony down on its backside with a thump. Quick as a flash, it jumped up and set off across the beautifully kept garden. If you have never seen the damage a loose pony can do to a garden in a short time, then you really wouldn't believe it...

Well, I had been in this situation before, and knew that it was no good me trying to catch it, as it was me it was running away from, so I walked quietly round the path, well away from the pony, and closed the gate which opened onto the road, and then went and rang the doorbell, and informed the owner that the pony was loose in the garden. She went and got a bucket with a few nuts in and caught it easily enough, but when I tied it up again with a fresh rope it set about that one as it had done the first one, and, having had success already, it was even more determined to get away again; and it did — straight across the garden again! The owner went and caught it again, and held onto it whilst I got its feet done. As long as she was with it, it didn't bother.

Next time I went, I remembered the fiasco from the time before, and thought, *Right, we're not having that lot again.* So I got *both* my own head collars and ropes out (I always carried my own) and used them both to tie the older pony with. Well, it tried to break away again, and oh, how it tried, but it couldn't get away this time. After a while, it saw the light, and I was able to trim its feet without too much bother. Each time I went after that, I used two head collars, and had no more trouble; it even stopped trying to get away, until one day, one of the daughters was home, and when I arrived, she had both ponies tied up in the yard, but with only one head collar on, and was grooming them.

I got my toolbox out and apron on, and approached the nearest pony (which happened to be the older one). Straight away, it pulled back, broke the rope and set off across the garden. The daughter duly went and caught it and brought it back, and said, 'I've never seen it do that before,' so I told her of the past performances, and said it needed two ties.

I put both my tying up pieces on it, and right away it stood without any further trouble. However, when the girl came to loosen it off, she undid one rope, and was about to undo the other, when the pony pulled back again. It knew there was only one rope holding it, and thought, *Now's my chance!* — or something like that — and tried to break away once more. Fortunately, my rope held long enough to loosen the slip knot before the pony managed to break it. That pony knew when it had a chance to get away, *and* when it didn't. Who said ponies can't reason?

Fashion

I had shod one particular horse two or three times, and to the best of my knowledge, there had never been any problems. When I arrived on this particular day, the owner, a girl about fifteen years old, asked me if I would shoe it with feathered heels. I asked her what sort of problems she had been having, and she replied, 'No problems, I just want feathered heels.' I explained to her that if there were no problems — like brushing, or cutting into itself — then feathered heels were totally unnecessary, and would take away valuable heel support, which would be bad for the horse. 'Well, I want it shoeing with feathered heels,' she said.

Now, as you have probably already guessed, this young lady was the only child of a wealthy family, and was used to having her own way, and she wasn't used to having *no* for an answer. But somebody has to look out for the good of the horse, so I explained once more, as patiently as I could, that if these shoes were not necessary for surgical reasons, then they could only do the horse harm, because the feet need as much heel support as they can get. It made no difference; she still wanted the feathered heels. I then asked her if she knew what these feathered heels actually were. 'Well, no,' she said, 'but I read about them in a magazine and I want them on my horse.'

By this time I had had about enough of this precious little madam, and I said to her, 'Now look, I have explained to you twice why these shoes are bad for your horse, and this is not Freeman, Hardy and Willis's, where you can choose whatever takes your fancy. I'm not going to help you to lame your horse, so you either have ordinary shoes, which are all it needs, or you can get it done somewhere else.'

Well, she needed the horse for some activity or other, so I shod it up for her as normal, but she never rang again. I often wondered if she ever got her feathered heels... I know what *she* needed!

The Mother and Daughter

I attended at a particular livery place for many years, and during that time I shod all sorts of horses and ponies, from Clydesdale to Shetland, and all sizes in between. Some were good to do, some were not so good to do, but I don't remember ever having one animal that I had to leave without shoes because of bad behaviour. The owner of the yard would tie one up to be shod, and bring at least one more so that there were always two or more horses or ponies together for company. As I've said, this is important when they are used to each other's company, and it tends to reduce bad behaviour, and anything that does that is most welcome. I would then be left alone to get on with doing my job as I saw fit without any interference, which is something else that I think is important. Then the yard owner would come out every hour or so and take one away, and bring another to take its place.

On this particular day, there was a new horse to be shod, and the owner, a girl of about fourteen, and her mother were there with it. I asked them to tie it up and come back in a good half-hour, and I should be just about done by then. 'No,' said the daughter, 'I am staying and holding it, as it hasn't been shod before, and it's only three years old, and I don't want it spoiling.'

Whenever anyone has said that to me in the past, it has always been a sure sign that it is already spoiled. People seem to think that horses are broken in by giving them a sugar lump, patting them and saying, 'Aaawww, he's a good boy' – or girl, as the case might be – ignoring the fact that they need handling for as many hours a week as they can manage, and in a lot of cases, more than that. I asked the daughter if she had been picking its feet up and tapping them. She looked a bit vacant and said no, she hadn't. I thought, *That figures…*

Anyway, I made a start, and sure enough, it didn't want to know. It lashed out, pulled back, reared and jumped sideways – both away from me and at me – and it was obviously going to be a job where I could have done without the owners there. After I'd tried to hold on and tap its feet, it showed no sign of cooperating, so I thumped it a couple of times.

Well, the daughter started shouting at me, telling me how cruel I was, and that she had to have it done quietly. So I asked her if she would tell the horse that it had to be done quietly.

'Don't be so daft,' she said, 'I can't tell the horse!'

I said to her, 'I'm not going to be spoken to like that by a bit of a kid, and if you had done your homework on it, there would have been no trouble.'

'I'm not a bit of a kid!' she shouted.

'As far as I'm concerned, you are a bit of a kid, and don't talk to me like that,' I retorted.

'Well, I'm not having you thump my horse,' she repeated.

'No,' I replied, 'and your horse isn't going to thump me, either, so just keep quiet and hold onto it, and it won't come to any harm. Someone's got to teach it how to behave, as you haven't made a very good job of it, and I don't have all day to do what you should have already done.'

With that I went for the twitch (a small noose attached to the horse's lip). Now, I don't like using the twitch (some bright spark has invented the name 'humane twitch'), but owners seem to think it is acceptable for their horses to stand for ages with their noses screwed up. To me, it always seemed less cruel to give the horse a good thumping, which takes about three seconds, when the horse may need the twitch on for half an hour. But cruelty is a bit like beauty – it's in the eye of the beholder – and of course, with the twitch, you are not actually seen to be being violent. Anyway the girl started screaming that she wasn't having that either, so I told her she would have to have either one or the other, keep quiet and hold onto the horse, go away and let me get on, or take the horse away altogether. She decided to take the horse away.

Now, all this time the mother had kept out of things, but I thought that anytime now I'd catch a packet off her. I looked at her and she was smiling. I thought that a bit odd after falling out with her daughter. She looked at me and said, 'Thank you, it's time someone told that little madam where to get off! She's never been spoken to like that in her life before.'

I really couldn't believe what I was hearing, but I told her that she was fifty per cent responsible for that. 'It's no good me saying anything to her,' the mother said, 'she just runs to her father and he gives in to her all the time. If I send her home and bring the horse back, will you shoe it for me?'

'It's all right to me,' I answered, 'but you do know the score, don't you?'

'I don't think you'll do anything that isn't necessary,' she said, and off she went for the horse.

You may not believe this, but the horse didn't move again, and I had it done in quick sticks. 'Will you shoe it in future if I see to it?' the mother asked.

I said I would, and she came each time for the next three or four times. Then the daughter started coming again, and we continued with our rather frosty relationship, which took a few years to heal; but heal it did, in the end.

No Worse Reason

This is a story about a chap who was a small business owner, with no equestrian background (he knew nothing about horses), but who wanted to get his daughter into showjumping. He bought a pony whilst the daughter was still quite young, and as she progressed, he bought a slightly better performer, until she became quite an accomplished competitor on the junior showjumping circuit. I had shod for him throughout this transformation period, until one day when I went, I found he had acquired two new 14.2 jumping ponies. I commented that he was getting a bit ambitious, and he said that yes, they were going to do some winning now that the daughter had got some experience.

Over the next few visits the owner seemed quite happy with his daughter's progress, and it appeared that she was indeed doing some winning. One day I went and discovered he had bought a Shetland pony. I asked why he had bought it, and he said he thought it would be a companion to the jumping ponies.

All went well, until I went one day and he said that he wanted the Shetland shoeing. Well, some of my worst injuries have come from shoeing Shetlands. I have had my legs pierced with nails and chunks taken out of them, I have had pieces taken out of my finger ends with the clenches, I have had my trouser legs torn from the knee down to the floor, and I have even had my leather apron ripped — so Shetland shoeing is not one of my favourite pastimes. I managed to talk him out of it, convincing him that a small pony needed to be doing a lot of roadwork before it needed shoes on. Anyway, the next time I went, he again asked for the Shetland shoeing, and I tried once more to talk him out of it — but he was adamant, so I asked why he thought it needed shoes on.

'Well, the horses are always kicking it, and if it has shoes on, it will be able to kick them back,' was the astonishing reply.

'I can think of no worse reason than that to have shoes on anything,' I told him, 'and what's more, it will be a very difficult job — one that I think we should not even start on.'

'What's the matter with you?' he asked. 'A thing that size can't be a problem.'

I told him that it could be a bigger problem than he could even imagine, but there was no changing his mind, so I thought, *Right! You've asked for it, so you can have it.*

Although there was a tying-up ring available, I said he would have to hold the pony whilst I worked on it. 'That's no problem,' he said, so we got started. I always started with the hind feet, and when I asked for the first one, it kicked, jumped sideways and tried to squash me against the wall, but I got the hind feet trimmed ready for fitting shoes, and then started on the front feet. Straight away, it reared up and went for the owner with front feet flailing like wind-mills. Fortunately he managed to dodge the onslaught, but he was a bit shaken by the experience, and said, 'I didn't expect that.'

I said that I had warned him that it would be difficult, but that he had insisted.

'How did you know it would be that bad?' he asked.

I told him that the trouble with most small ponies, and Shetlands in particular, is that they are never broken in or handled like horses are. People sit a kid on its back, and if it doesn't chuck it off, then it is considered broken in. They also have very short legs, which are extremely difficult to hold onto. So they have the advantage there too, as they can so easily throw you off balance, and as soon as they find a way of getting away, they will exploit it to the full.

'I think we will not bother shoeing it after all,' the owner concluded — I couldn't have agreed more.

The author, about to shoe another Shetland pony.

Leaning

For many years prior to retirement, I would often hear a customer say, 'I don't know how you manage to do that job so easily, it nearly kills me just picking feet out.' So I used to tell them that it wasn't always like that, and I had the same difficulty as anybody else in days gone by.

I remember one big black horse in particular that didn't so much lean on me as sit on me. I had just started horse shoeing, and after the initial period of watching, I was given the task of clenching-up. I remember well how hard I found this task, and my legs would ache fit to drop off after just one foot; and of course, there were three more to go at.

This was in the early 1950s when there were very few horses about where I worked. There were only a few riding horses at that time, as horse-riding was not yet popular, and the farmers were changing to tractors, so there were not many workhorses to shoe either. In fact, much of our time was spent taking shafts off horse-drawn farm implements, and making and fitting drawbars. I have made a drawbar for virtually every type of horse-drawn implement: ploughs, hay rakers, turners, block carts, flat carts – you name it, I have made a drawbar for it.

The point of this digression is to say that the horse was very much in the decline in those days, and at our forge, we would only shoe about seven or eight horses a week, which didn't do much for getting 'muscled up', and I found the work very hard indeed. Of course, after the upsurge in riding horses in the late Sixties and early Seventies, things became very different, and when I became self-employed, I would shoe between eight and ten by myself every day, and soon got 'muscled up'.

To get back to the intended story about that big black horse, when I was clenching-up the hind shoes, the horse would drop its body onto my back, and put more and more weight on, until, with thigh muscles bursting, I would jump out from under, and the horse would fall on the floor. My employer would say, 'Can't ta hod it? A young chap like thee, wot's up wi' thi?' This would make me a bit ashamed, because he was turned sixty, but he had been through the mill and knew how to deal with this situation. But he never told *me* how to deal with it.

It wasn't until many years later that I found out. As there aren't many real 'liggers on' like that one, you don't get a lot of practice at dealing with the problem. I found out that if you give them something to sit on, they will sit, and the more you try to hold them, the more they will sit on you, and really make your life a misery. The trick is, as soon as they start to drop on you, you have to shift your backside out of the way, so that you are standing virtually sideways on. Even with your backside out of the way, you can still feel the horse dropping to find something to sit on. This puts a lot of strain on the thigh muscles, but at least you can get the job done without having to jump out from under, and risk being squashed under the falling horse, or save getting pushed into the ground like a fence post. This is why farriers seem to do the job so easily, because it's these hard horses that make the ordinary ones seem easy.

Fenced In

This story concerns an episode in the young life of a horse that I went on to shoe for over twenty years.

I remember it being born, as I shod its mother for quite a few years before she became a brood mare. It was chestnut, with long legs and large knees, and looked like making the big hunter that the family were hoping for, as hunting was a large part of their winter life. The foal was also quite precocious, and didn't see why mere humans should handle it; and although the owners were very experienced horse people, they found this foal very difficult to deal with.

It didn't want to have a halter on, and when the owner managed to get one on, the foal would shake its head, pull back and rear, and would try to knock the halter off by striking at it with its front feet; and if anyone was in the way — tough! It wouldn't allow anyone to even touch it, or it would whip round and give them a double barrel. I suppose this behaviour is quite normal for a young foal, but the trouble with this one was that it went on and on and showed no sign of getting any more amenable.

The time came when I was asked to trim its feet. Well, that was a rodeo. It kicked, reared, pulled, pushed and jumped, and I had great difficulty even holding onto its feet, never mind trimming them; but I managed to do a bit of foot tapping, and had a quick rasp round on each foot. I was asked to trim its feet about every two months, and it got no better for going on two years. By this time it had grown considerably, which made the job of foot dressing even more difficult.

Slowly the work done on it by its owners began to get through to it, and its behaviour gradually got better... and then it was shoeing time. It would stand quite well for a while, then it would decide that it had had enough, and would start pulling and pushing and jumping about, but I always managed to hold on and get the shoes on.

One day when I was shoeing it, it got to the 'had enough' stage, and pulled back and managed to escape. It whipped round, jumped over the garden wall and shot across the lawn and through a small gap in the hedge. How it had come to identify this as an escape route is a mystery, because it wasn't so much a gap, as the leylandii were just a fraction wider apart, and it didn't look wide enough for a horse to get through. But get through it did. There was a leylandii hedge down one side, and a fence down the other side, and a passage in between about twenty yards long, starting three feet wide at the entrance, and tapering off to a point where the hedge and fence met.

Well, the horse went as far as it could get down this passage, and then became stuck — it couldn't go forward, nor could it turn round, and as the passage was so narrow, the owner couldn't get into it. So the family had a meeting, and decided that the only thing to do was to cut a tree down, and lead the horse out and back through the garden. This they proceeded to do, and I finally got the job done. The next time I went, the gap in the hedge had been securely fenced off.

As the horse hunted more, its behaviour improved considerably, and it and I had a good relationship for the next twenty years.

A Dangerous Game

In my early days of self-employment, I was quite often called upon to dress cows' feet. This operation could turn out to be anything between straightforward to downright dangerous.

In the early 1950s when I first became involved in this side of farriery, the job of cow's foot dressing always seemed to be quite easy, and I can remember when a farmer would bring a cow to the smithy in a cattle wagon or a trailer, and we would dress its feet in the truck. We would wrap a sack round a leg just below the hock and, with one man at each side, we would lift the leg, and a third man would do the actual trimming. There never seemed to be any difficulty with this method, as the animals always seemed to accept the procedure. I suppose that in those days the cattle were actually handled quite regularly and used to human proximity, being tied by a neck chain twice a day for milking, and having their udders washed. Quite a lot were still being milked by hand then, and even those which were being machine-milked were still tied up throughout the milking.

Then came the milking parlour. The cows were no longer tied up during milking, but driven into a herring-bone parlour where they stood loose, and given a feed whilst the milking process took place. This procedure led to the cows not being in such close contact with people, as they were milked from a pit, and I came to notice the change in behaviour when dressing their feet, which took place from this time.

Also at this time, cattle crushes were almost unheard of, but to dress the feet, the cattle had to be tied up somehow, or they would just walk off when they'd had enough. So, I used to look for a place in a mistal, with an old-fashioned tie-stake and a roof beam overhead to tie the leg up to. I would tie a rope round the hock and lift the leg, and someone (usually the farmer) would hold onto the loose end of the rope whilst I got on with the trimming. Quite often I would get the job done easily. Sometimes the cow would struggle a bit, but some, that really didn't want to have their feet dressed, would lash out with both hind feet every few seconds, and this is when the job became dangerous. You see, when a cow kicks out, it can reach five feet at least behind it, so anyone standing less than six feet away was in danger of being felled by these vicious kicks. It wasn't so bad for the farrier, as he could feel the kicks coming, and all he had to do was step aside and let the cow get on with it, then step in again when the tantrum was over, and carry on trimming until the next assault took place.

I was doing a beast of this sort one day, and it was as bad as any I have ever seen. The farmer, who should have known better, kept walking back and forth behind the cow, and I was getting a bit worried for his safety. I said to him, 'I wish you wouldn't walk across behind this cow like that, you might just catch one.'

He always stood with his thumbs in his waistcoat armholes, as he was doing at this time, and said, 'I've been with beeas' [beasts] all my life, don't tell me what I can do and what I can't.'

Anyway, he did it once too often, and the cow hit him with both hind feet just under the breastbone, and dropped him — out cold on the floor. He never recovered from that blow — as I have written. It can be a dangerous game.

Fortunately, these days there are special crushes in which cows are fastened, turned over, and their feet tied to stakes, so that these incidents no longer need to occur.

There was another similar incident at somewhere near the time of the above story. I was doing a cow's feet at a farm, and it happened to be milking time. I was working in the first stall in a 'seven 'oyle' (three double stands and one single) just inside the door.

The cow that I was working on was one of the 'don't like it' brigade, and would lash out every now and again. The farmer's man appeared in the doorway carrying a milking machine in each hand. Just as he entered, the cow lashed out and dropped him, with a clatter of machinery. The poor lad didn't know what had hit him, but I bet he was sore for quite a while — yes, a dangerous game!

The Bull

A farmer rang to ask if I would go to his place to trim the feet of an Aberdeen Angus bull. He said that if I could give him a few dates and times, he would arrange with his vet to come and knock it out and then let me know when to go.

The vet and I arrived at about the same time, and as he prepared the injection, the vet told me that I had approximately half an hour to get the job done before the bull recovered from the knockout drops. He duly administered the dose and waited until it took effect, then off he went, leaving me to get on with the foot dressing.

Unfortunately, the bull dropped rather close to the wall, leaving me with very little space in which to work, and I thought, *If this big b— comes round whilst I am working on it, it'll squash me against the wall like a fly, because there's no way out!* Anyway, the job had to be done and there was no time to lose, as half an hour isn't all that long to do a job of that magnitude. So I got to work as best I could in the confined space between bull and wall, and managed to get three feet done.

I had just made a start on the fourth foot, when the bull gave a groan and heaved itself up from flat out, to a lying down position. As soon as I felt the bull move, I jumped straight over it in a single leap, otherwise I would have been squashed, as it was right hard up against the wall by the time it was in the normal lying-down position.

Aberdeen Angus bulls don't look very big when you see them in a field, but when you get close to them they are massive, with huge bodies and short legs. I don't think that I could have leapt over an obstacle of that size if I had consciously tried, but I cleared it with room to spare in my desperation to avoid being trapped. I had no choice but to call the job complete with three and a half feet dressed, but there was no way on earth that I was going to finish the fourth.

The Cows

I was shoeing for a customer one day, when her father came out of the house and asked me if I would dress his cows' feet. He was a businessman who had bought a farm so that his daughter could do horses, and he could do farming. He was not a farmer by any stretch of the imagination, but he had decided that he was going to rear pedigree cattle. He had a herd of about twenty Welsh Blacks, which did nothing but eat and breed, and they spent all their lives out in a field.

I asked first of all if he had a cattle crush. No, he hadn't. I then asked where we could do them. 'Where do you usually do these jobs?' he asked.

'We will need to have them inside where they can be tied up under a roof-beam, so that we can rope a leg up to work on,' I told him.

'That's OK, we'll drive them into the mistal and you can do them wherever you want,' was the confident reply.

'Have they ever been in a mistal?' I asked.

'Not that I know of,' he answered.

'I think you will have a bit of difficulty getting them in if they're not used to it,' I said.

'Oh — they're stone quiet,' he assured me, 'I'll have them in ready when you come to do them.'

I thought, *Aye, they're all stone quiet when they are out in a field eating, but it'll be a different kettle of fish when you get them inside — if you get them inside…*

Anyway, the chap was confident, and as with many of my other stories, the owners of these animals always knew better than I did. Although I have been in these situations many times before, I have found it best to let them have their own way, as they seem to learn better by experience.

I arrived to do the job, and sure enough, he had them penned in the yard, milling round and making a right racket. 'I can't get them to go into the mistal,' he said, so I reminded him that they were supposed to be stone quiet and totally amenable.

'Well, they are normally... I don't know what's matter with them today,' he said.

'They've never been inside before, that's what's the matter with them,' I told him, 'and I can't possibly do them out in the yard without a crush.'

'I didn't expect all this trouble,' he said, 'I think we'd better leave them.'

'Yes,' I agreed, 'judging by the state they've worked themselves up into, I think that is a good idea.'

I just hoped that none of the feet really needed dressing.

The Dulux Dog

It was snowing quite heavily when I arrived at a fine place to shoe two riding ponies. It was a great big house, set in its own grounds of at least an acre, surrounded by high walls and trees. There was an old stable block with a small courtyard, but nowhere suitable to shoe the ponies under cover, so the job was to do outside, whatever the weather.

Not only was it snowing heavily, but the wind was howling like a demented banshee, and driving the snow horizontally across the small yard. My helper, the young daughter of the household, and the rider of the ponies, had to stand and hold them, as there was nowhere to tie them up. I have always maintained that standing holding horses in bad weather is the worst job in the world, because the holder can only get colder, and in this case wetter, as the job progresses. I asked the girl if she thought that she would be all right with the clothes she was already wearing. She said she would, so I donned thick jumper and waterproof gilet, and got cracking with the job of shoeing the ponies.

The biggest trouble with being a travelling farrier is that you are stuck with whatever facilities — or lack of facilities — are available; and if the weather is nasty, you either get cold and wet, or you leave the job without pay. And to me, that was never an option. So we got wet!

I finished the first pony and was about to start on the second one, when I noticed that the girl was shivering a bit. I asked her if she wanted to go to the house for another coat or a warm-up, but she said that she would be all right. I went into my van and brought out a new car coat which a customer, who manufactured them, had given me, and which I had not worn yet, and wrapped it round her. The hem of the coat reached almost to the ground, the collar just about covered her head and the sleeves reached to below her knees, so that I felt a bit better about her welfare for the next forty-five minutes, whilst I shod the second pony.

All went well until I had nearly finished, when the girl's mother came out of the house to pay me. Unfortunately, an Old English sheepdog (a Dulux dog) came out with her, with huge hairy paws and hair trailing on the ground in all the muddy slush. It came lolloping across the yard through all this muck, and jumped straight up onto the girl, depositing a large helping of mud all over my new coat.

I was a bit miffed. The mother asked how much I wanted for the shoeing, so I told her and added a fiver for the cleaning. Neither mother nor daughter offered any apology for the mess, or thanks for using my coat to keep the daughter warm; but I don't suppose you do these things for thanks, although they would be appreciated.

Someone to Watch Over Me

I had arranged to shoe two horses for a customer at eight o'clock one morning. At this place I had to shoe the horses outside the field gate on some railway sleepers, which formed a bridge over a ditch at the side of a fairly quiet road. If the weather was wet there was no shelter, and the job was to do in the rain or snow, and, as two horses would take one and a half hours to shoe, it could be quite unpleasant. However, on the previous evening, another customer rang to ask if I could shoe two at a place further away.

It has always been my practice to start with the farthest away, and work my way home, in as straight a line as possible. This cuts travelling time during working hours, and is also more economical than running about the countryside willy-nilly.

I rang the first customer and explained the situation, and asked if she minded me coming to her two hours later, at ten o'clock. She had no objections, so I went to the farthest away job first the following morning. At eight o'clock it was raining heavily, but at this place it didn't matter, because I could shoe under cover, and I got the job done without getting wet. I set off from there, dreading the next couple of hours' shoeing in the rain.

When I arrived at the next place, as soon as I jumped out of my motor, the rain stopped, and I shod the two horses outside without getting wet − for which I was quite grateful; but as soon as I set off, the heavens opened again, and the rain poured down until dinnertime. I looked up to the sky and whispered a quiet 'thank you' to whoever was watching over me that morning.

On another occasion, I had a horse to shoe at a very exposed location, another place where there was no shelter from the elements. I had just got started when I looked down the valley and saw a big rain cloud coming towards us. I asked the young woman who owned the horse if she had a raincoat with her. 'Why do you ask that?' she asked, so I pointed at the cloud and said, 'Well, we look like getting a soaking any time now.'

I always had plenty of coats and jumpers with me, so I knew that I would be all right, and I also had a large coat that the owner could wear if necessary.

The storm arrived, but passed us by about twenty yards away. We could see the rain bouncing off the road, and could hear it sort of rustling and splashing, but we stayed dry as the storm passed through, and we watched it disappear over the hill — it was quite eerie. Once again I whispered my grateful thanks to whoever was watching over me.

In the End...

I hope you have enjoyed reading these tales. They are a condensed version of my life as a travelling farrier over the last thirty years. These stories are about situations which actually took place in my everyday life. What makes these so special and worth writing about are the conversations that actually took place, against the antics of the animals concerned.

My working life can be divided into three main parts. The first five years were spent as an apprentice; the following eighteen years, as an industrial blacksmith; and the final thirty years as a travelling farrier. I think that the last thirty were the best years because I seemed to have found my niche in life, and generally enjoyed the rigours of the nomadic farrier.

I covered a rather large area during my years on the road; from Huddersfield through Halifax, Bradford and Leeds right to the A1, south of Wetherby. I also had a thriving business round Ripon and Boroughbridge, which lasted for many years, but my main areas were south Bradford and north Leeds.

My career was brought to an abrupt end, as mentioned in the Introduction, with a road accident that wrecked my trailer. This was a consequence of a vehicle being parked on a blind bend on a steep hill down which I was driving, and a Land Rover and trailer overtaking it at far too great a speed. By the time I could see the Land Rover it was too late to stop, and I had to either take the Land Rover or the wall. I chose the wall, and smashed my trailer up beyond repair. So that was that!

I was not particularly sorry that my shoeing career had come to an end, as I had felt for some time that I should give up whilst I was still in good physical health. Another decisive factor was the direction in which farriery seemed to be heading. We seem to be losing the ability to use our knowledge of limb anatomy to assess a situation using good old 'signs and symptoms' which have stood the craft in good stead for many years. Instead, the customer is made to pay through the nose for X-rays and nerve blocks, which in many cases are totally unnecessary. But of course, there is money to be made out of these techniques — 'nuff said.

I have now been retired for two and a half years and live a happy, busy life in the outskirts of Keighley. I drive for the local Community Transport Service; I walk every day, look after my rather large garden and play bowls several times a week. I have taken two courses of computer studies and become quite a competent typist. In fact, it was learning to use a computer that triggered off the urge to write these stories. I don't think I would ever have started otherwise.

Thank you for reading my book. I hope you have found it interesting, humorous, educational, human and caring, amongst other emotions — not necessarily in that order — because that's how it is intended to be; and please recommend it to a friend.

Before I close, I would like to present a few approximate statistics that you may find of interest. During my travelling career, I covered half a million miles, used a quarter of a million shoes, scrapped thirty tons of used shoes and used one and three quarter million nails! I wish I could see that lot in a pile — it would be some sight…

Printed in the United Kingdom
by Lightning Source UK Ltd.
107363UKS00001B/106